May 1, 2014

DEAR MR. PRESIDENT:

We are living in the midst of a social, economic, and technological revolution. How we communicate, socialize, spend leisure time, and conduct business has moved onto the Internet. The Internet has in turn moved into our phones, into devices spreading around our homes and cities, and into the factories that power the industrial economy. The resulting explosion of data and discovery is changing our world.

In January, you asked us to conduct a 90-day study to examine how big data will transform the way we live and work and alter the relationships between government, citizens, businesses, and consumers. This review focuses on how the public and private sectors can maximize the benefits of big data while minimizing its risks. It also identifies opportunities for big data to grow our economy, improve health and education, and make our nation safer and more energy efficient.

While big data unquestionably increases the potential of government power to accrue unchecked, it also hold within it solutions that can enhance accountability, privacy, and the rights of citizens. Properly implemented, big data will become an historic driver of progress, helping our nation perpetuate the civic and economic dynamism that has long been its hallmark.

Big data technologies will be transformative in every sphere of life. The knowledge discovery they make possible raises considerable questions about how our framework for privacy protection applies in a big data ecosystem. Big data also raises other concerns. A significant finding of this report is that big data analytics have the potential to eclipse longstanding civil rights protections in how personal information is used in housing, credit, employment, health, education, and the marketplace. Americans' relationship with data should expand, not diminish, their opportunities and potential.

We are building the future we will inherit. The United States is better suited than any nation on earth to ensure the digital revolution continues to work for individual empowerment and social good. We are pleased to present this report's recommendations on how we can embrace big data technologies while at the same time protecting fundamental values like privacy, fairness, and self-determination. We are committed to the initiatives and reforms it proposes. The dialogue we set in motion today will help us remain true to our values even as big data reshapes the world around us.

JOHN PODESTA
Counselor to the President

PENNY PRITZKER
Secretary of Commerce

ERNEST J. MONIZ
Secretary of Energy

JOHN HOLDREN
Director, Office of Science & Technology Policy

JEFFREY ZIENTS
Director, National Economic Council

Table of Contents

I. Big Data and the Individual

What is Big Data?

Since the first censuses were taken and crop yields recorded in ancient times, data collection and analysis have been essential to improving the functioning of society. Foundational work in calculus, probability theory, and statistics in the 17th and 18th centuries provided an array of new tools used by scientists to more precisely predict the movements of the sun and stars and determine population-wide rates of crime, marriage, and suicide. These tools often led to stunning advances. In the 1800s, Dr. John Snow used early modern data science to map cholera "clusters" in London. By tracing to a contaminated public well a disease that was widely thought to be caused by "miasmatic" air, Snow helped lay the foundation for the germ theory of disease.[1]

Gleaning insights from data to boost economic activity also took hold in American industry. Frederick Winslow Taylor's use of a stopwatch and a clipboard to analyze productivity at Midvale Steel Works in Pennsylvania increased output on the shop floor and fueled his belief that data science could revolutionize every aspect of life.[2] In 1911, Taylor wrote *The Principles of Scientific Management* to answer President Theodore Roosevelt's call for increasing "national efficiency":

> [T]he fundamental principles of scientific management are applicable to all kinds of human activities, from our simplest individual acts to the work of our great corporations.... [W]henever these principles are correctly applied, results must follow which are truly astounding.[3]

Today, data is more deeply woven into the fabric of our lives than ever before. We aspire to use data to solve problems, improve well-being, and generate economic prosperity. The collection, storage, and analysis of data is on an upward and seemingly unbounded trajectory, fueled by increases in processing power, the cratering costs of computation and storage, and the growing number of sensor technologies embedded in devices of all kinds. In 2011, some estimated the amount of information created and replicated would

---

[1] Scott Crosier, *John Snow: The London Cholera Epidemic of 1854*, Center for Spatially Integrated Social Science, University of California, Santa Barbara, 2007, http://www.csiss.org/classics/content/8.
[2] Simon Head, *The New Ruthless Economy: Work and Power in the Digital Age*, (Oxford University Press, 2005).
[3] Frederick Taylor, *The Principles of Scientific Management* (Harper & Brothers, 1911), p. 7, http://www.eldritchpress.org/fwt/ti.html.

surpass 1.8 zettabytes.[4] In 2013, estimates reached 4 zettabytes of data generated worldwide.[5]

What is a Zettabyte?

A zettabyte is 1,000 000,000,000,000,000,000 bytes, or units of information. Consider that a single byte equals one character of text. The 1,250 pages of Leo Tolstoy's *War and Peace* would fit into a zettabyte 323 trillion times.[6] Or imagine that every person in the United States took a digital photo every second of every day for over a month. All of those photos put together would equal about one zettabyte.

More than 500 million photos are uploaded and shared every day, along with more than 200 hours of video every minute. But the volume of information that people create themselves—the full range of communications from voice calls, emails and texts to uploaded pictures, video, and music—pales in comparison to the amount of digital information created *about* them each day.

These trends will continue. We are only in the very nascent stage of the so-called "Internet of Things," when our appliances, our vehicles and a growing set of "wearable" technologies will be able to communicate with each other. Technological advances have driven down the cost of creating, capturing, managing, and storing information to one-sixth of what it was in 2005. And since 2005, business investment in hardware, software, talent, and services has increased as much as 50 percent, to $4 trillion.

The "Internet of Things"

The "Internet of Things" is a term used to describe the ability of devices to communicate with each other using embedded sensors that are linked through wired and wireless networks. These devices could include your thermostat, your car, or a pill you swallow so the doctor can monitor the health of your digestive tract. These connected devices use the Internet to transmit, compile, and analyze data.

There are many definitions of "big data" which may differ depending on whether you are a computer scientist, a financial analyst, or an entrepreneur pitching an idea to a venture capitalist. Most definitions reflect the growing technological ability to capture, aggregate, and process an ever-greater volume, velocity, and variety of data. In other words, "data is now available faster, has greater coverage and scope, and includes new types of observations and measurements that previously were not available."[7] More precisely, big

---

[4] John Gantz and David Reinsel, *Extracting Value from Chaos,* IDC, 2011, http://www.emc.com/collateral/analyst-reports/idc-extracting-value-from-chaos-ar.pdf.
[5] Mary Meeker and Liang Yu, *Internet Trends*, Kleiner Perkins Caulfield Byers, 2013, http://www.slideshare.net/kleinerperkins/kpcb-internet-trends-2013.
[6] "2016: The Year of the Zettabyte," Daily Infographic, March 23, 2013, http://dailyinfographic.com/2016-the-year-of-the-zettabyte-infographic.
[7] Liran Einav and Jonathan Levin, "The Data Revolution and Economic Analysis," Working Paper, No. 19035, *National Bureau of Economic Research*, 2013, http://www.nber.org/papers/w19035; Viktor Mayer-

datasets are "large, diverse, complex, longitudinal, and/or distributed datasets generated from instruments, sensors, Internet transactions, email, video, click streams, and/or all other digital sources available today and in the future."[8]

What really matters about big data is what it does. Aside from how we define big data as a technological phenomenon, the wide variety of potential uses for big data analytics raises crucial questions about whether our legal, ethical, and social norms are sufficient to protect privacy and other values in a big data world. Unprecedented computational power and sophistication make possible unexpected discoveries, innovations, and advancements in our quality of life. But these capabilities, most of which are not visible or available to the average consumer, also create an asymmetry of power between those who hold the data and those who intentionally or inadvertently supply it.

Part of the challenge, too, lies in understanding the many different contexts in which big data comes into play. Big data may be viewed as property, as a public resource, or as an expression of individual identity.[9] Big data applications may be the driver of America's economic future or a threat to cherished liberties. Big data may be all of these things. For the purposes of this 90-day study, the review group does not purport to have all the answers to big data. Both the technology of big data and the industries that support it are constantly innovating and changing. Instead, the study focuses on asking the most important questions about the relationship between individuals and those who collect and use data about them.

The Scope of This Review

On January 17, in a speech at the Justice Department about reforming the United States' signals intelligence practices, President Obama tasked his Counselor John Podesta with leading a comprehensive review of the impact big data technologies are having, and will have, on a range of economic, social, and government activities. Podesta was joined in this effort by Secretary of Commerce Penny Pritzker, Secretary of Energy Ernest Moniz, the President's Science Advisor John Holdren, the President's Economic Advisor Jeffrey Zients, and other senior government officials. The President's Council of Advisors for Science & Technology conducted a parallel report to take measure of the underlying technologies. Their findings underpin many of the technological assertions in this report.

This review was conceived as fundamentally a scoping exercise. Over 90 days, the review group engaged with academic experts, industry representatives, privacy advocates,

---

Schonberger and Kenneth Cukier, *Big Data: A Revolution That Will Transform How We Live, Work, and Think*, (Houghton Mifflin Harcourt, 2013).

[8] National Science Foundation, Solicitation 12-499: *Core Techniques and Technologies for Advancing Big Data Science & Engineering (BIGDATA)*, 2012, http://www.nsf.gov/pubs/2012/nsf12499/nsf12499.pdf.

[9] Harvard Professor of Science & Technology Studies Sheila Jasanoff argues that framing the policy implications of big data is difficult precisely because it manifests in multiple contexts that each call up different operative concerns, including big data as property (who owns it); big data as common pool resources (who manages it and on what principles); and big data as identity (it is us ourselves, and thus its management raises constitutional questions about rights).

civil rights groups, law enforcement agents, and other government agencies. The White House Office of Science and Technology Policy jointly organized three university conferences, at the Massachusetts Institute of Technology, New York University, and the University of California, Berkeley. The White House Office of Science & Technology Policy also issued a "Request for Information" seeking public comment on issues of big data and privacy and received more than 70 responses. In addition, the WhiteHouse.gov platform was used to conduct an unscientific survey of public attitudes about different uses of big data and various big data technologies. A list of the working group's activities can be found in the Appendix.

What is Different about Big Data?

This chapter begins by defining what is truly new and different about big data, drawing on the work of the President's Council of Advisors on Science & Technology (PCAST), which has worked in parallel on a separate report, "Big Data and Privacy: A Technological Perspective."[10]

The "3 Vs": Volume, Variety and Velocity

For purposes of this study, the review group focused on data that is so large in volume, so diverse in variety or moving with such velocity, that traditional modes of data capture and analysis are insufficient—characteristics colloquially referred to as the "3 Vs." The declining cost of collection, storage, and processing of data, combined with new sources of data like sensors, cameras, geospatial and other observational technologies, means that we live in a world of near-ubiquitous data collection. The volume of data collected and processed is unprecedented. This explosion of data—from web-enabled appliances, wearable technology, and advanced sensors to monitor everything from vital signs to energy use to a jogger's running speed—will drive demand for high-performance computing and push the capabilities of even the most sophisticated data management technologies.

There is not only more data, but it also comes from a wider variety of sources and formats. As described in the report by the President's Council of Advisors of Science & Technology, some data is "born digital," meaning that it is created specifically for digital use by a computer or data processing system. Examples include email, web browsing, or GPS location. Other data is "born analog," meaning that it emanates from the physical world, but increasingly can be converted into digital format. Examples of analog data include voice or visual information captured by phones, cameras or video recorders, or physical activity data, such as heart rate or perspiration monitored by wearable devices.[11] With the rising capabilities of "data fusion," which brings together disparate sources of data, big data can lead to some remarkable insights.

---

[10] President's Council of Advisors on Science & Technology, *Big Data and Privacy: A Technological Perspective*, The White House, May 1, 2014.

[11] The distinction between data that is "born analog" and data that is "born digital" is explored at length in the PCAST report, *Big Data and Privacy*, p 18-22.

What are the sources of big data?

The sources and formats of data continue to grow in variety and complexity. A partial list of sources includes the public web; social media; mobile applications; federal, state and local records and databases; commercial databases that aggregate individual data from a spectrum of commercial transactions and public records; geospatial data; surveys; and traditional offline documents scanned by optical character recognition into electronic form. The advent of the more Internet-enabled devices and sensors expands the capacity to collect data from physical entities, including sensors and radio-frequency identification (RFID) chips. Personal location data can come from GPS chips, cell-tower triangulation of mobile devices, mapping of wireless networks, and in-person payments.[12]

Furthermore, data collection and analysis is being conducted at a velocity that is increasingly approaching real time, which means there is a growing potential for big data analytics to have an immediate effect on a person's surrounding environment or decisions being made about his or her life. Examples of high-velocity data include click-stream data that records users' online activities as they interact with web pages, GPS data from mobile devices that tracks location in real time, and social media that is shared broadly. Customers and companies are increasingly demanding that this data be analyzed to benefit them instantly. Indeed, a mobile mapping application is essentially useless if it cannot immediately and accurately identify the phone's location, and real-time processing is critical in the computer systems that ensure the safe operation of our cars.

New Opportunities, New Challenges

Big data technologies can derive value from large datasets in ways that were previously impossible—indeed, big data can generate insights that researchers didn't even think to seek. But the technical capabilities of big data have reached a level of sophistication and pervasiveness that demands consideration of how best to balance the opportunities afforded by big data against the social and ethical questions these technologies raise.

The power and opportunity of big data applications

Used well, big data analysis can boost economic productivity, drive improved consumer and government services, thwart terrorists, and save lives. Examples include:

- Big data and the growing "Internet of Things" have made it possible to merge the industrial and information economies. Jet engines and delivery trucks can now be outfitted with sensors that monitor hundreds of data points and send automatic

---

[12] See, e.g., Kapow Software, *Intelligence by Variety - Where to Find and Access Big Data*, http://www.kapowsoftware.com/resources/infographics/intelligence-by-variety-where-to-find-and-access-big-data.php; James Manyika, Michael Chui, Brad Brown, Jacques Bughin, Richard Dobbs, Charles Roxburgh, and Angela Hung Byers, *Big Data: The Next Frontier for Innovation, Competition, and Productivity,* McKinsey Global Institute, 2011, http://www.mckinsey.com/insights/business_technology/big_data_the_next_frontier_for_innovation.

alerts when maintenance is needed. [13] This makes repairs smoother, reducing maintenance costs and increasing safety.

- The Centers for Medicare and Medicaid Services have begun using predictive analytics software to flag likely instances of reimbursement fraud before claims are paid. The Fraud Prevention System helps identify the highest risk health care providers for fraud, waste and abuse in real time, and has already stopped, prevented or identified $115 million in fraudulent payments—saving $3 for every $1 spent in the program's first year. [14]

- During the most violent years of the war in Afghanistan, the Defense Advanced Research Projects Agency (DARPA) deployed teams of data scientists and visualizers to the battlefield. In a program called Nexus 7, these teams embedded directly with military units and used their tools to help commanders solve specific operational challenges. In one area, Nexus 7 engineers fused satellite and surveillance data to visualize how traffic flowed through road networks, making it easier to locate and destroy improvised explosive devices.

- One big data study synthesized millions of data samples from monitors in a neonatal intensive care unit to determine which newborns were likely to contract potentially fatal infections. By analyzing all of the data—not just what doctors noted on their rounds—the project was able to identify factors, like increases in temperature and heart rate, that serve as early warning signs that an infection may be taking root. These early signs of infection are not something even an experienced and attentive doctor would catch through traditional practices. [15]

Big data technology also holds tremendous promise for better managing demand across electricity grids, improving energy efficiency, boosting agricultural productivity in the developing world, and projecting the spread of infectious diseases, among other applications.

Finding the needle in the haystack

Computational capabilities now make "finding a needle in a haystack" not only possible, but practical. In the past, searching large datasets required both rationally organized data and a specific research question, relying on choosing the right query to return the correct result. Big data analytics enable data scientists to amass lots of data, including unstructured data, and find anomalies or patterns. A key privacy challenge in this model of

---

[13] Salesforce.com, "Collaboration helps GE Aviation bring its best inventions to life," http://www.salesforce.com/customers/stories/ge.jsp; Armand Gatdula, "Fleet Tracking Devices will be Installed in 22,000 UPS Trucks to Cut Costs and Improve Driver Efficiency in 2010," FieldLogix.com blog, July 20, 2010, http://www.fieldtechnologies.com/gps-tracking-systems-installed-in-ups-trucks-driver-efficiency.
[14] The Patient Protection and Affordable Care Act provides additional resources for fraud prevention. Centers for Medicare and Medicaid Services, "Fraud Prevention Toolkit," http://www.cms.gov/Outreach-and-Education/Outreach/Partnerships/FraudPreventionToolkit.html.
[15] IBM, "Smarter Healthcare in Canada: Redefining Value and Success," July 2012, http://www.ibm.com/smarterplanet/global/files/ca__en_us__health care__ca_brochure.pdf.

discovery is that in order to find the needle, you have to have a haystack. To obtain certain insights, you need a certain quantity of data.

For example, a genetic researcher at the Broad Institute found that having a large number of genetic datasets makes the critical difference in identifying the meaningful genetic variant for a disease. In this research, a genetic variant related to schizophrenia was not detectable when analyzed in 3,500 cases, and was only weakly identifiable using 10,000 cases, but was suddenly statistically significant with 35,000 cases. As the researcher observed, "There is an inflection point at which everything changes."[16] The need for vast quantities of data—particularly personally sensitive data like genetic data—is a significant challenge for researchers for a variety of reasons, but notably because of privacy laws that limit access to data.

The data clusters and relationships revealed in large data sets can be unexpected but deliver incisive results. On the other hand, even with lots of data, the information revealed by big data analysis isn't necessarily perfect. Identifying a pattern doesn't establish whether that pattern is significant. Correlation still doesn't equal causation. Finding a correlation with big data techniques may not be an appropriate basis for predicting outcomes or behavior, or rendering judgments on individuals. In big data, as with all data, interpretation is always important.

The benefits and consequences of perfect personalization

The fusion of many different kinds of data, processed in real time, has the power to deliver exactly the right message, product, or service to consumers before they even ask. Small bits of data can be brought together to create a clear picture of a person to predict preferences or behaviors. These detailed personal profiles and personalized experiences are effective in the consumer marketplace and can deliver products and offers to precise segments of the population—like a professional accountant with a passion for knitting, or a home chef with a penchant for horror films.

Unfortunately, "perfect personalization" also leaves room for subtle and not-so-subtle forms of discrimination in pricing, services, and opportunities. For example, one study found web searches involving black-identifying names (e.g., "Jermaine") were more likely to display ads with the word "arrest" in them than searches with white-identifying names (e.g., "Geoffrey"). This research was not able determine exactly why a racially biased result occurred, recognizing that ad display is algorithmically generated based on a number of variables and decision processes.[17] But it's clear that outcomes like these, by serving up different kinds of information to different groups, have the potential to

---

[16] Manolis Kellis, "Importance of Access to Large Populations," *Big Data Privacy Workshop: Advancing the State of the Art in Technology and Practice*, Cambridge, MA, March 3, 2014, http://web.mit.edu/bigdata-priv/ppt/ManolisKellis_PrivacyBigData_CSAIL-WH.pptx.
[17] Latanya Sweeney, "Discrimination in Online Ad Delivery," 2013, http://dataprivacylab.org/projects/onlineads/1071-1.pdf.

cause real harm to individuals, whether they are pursuing a job, purchasing a home, or simply searching for information.

Another concern is that big data technology could assign people to ideologically or culturally segregated enclaves known as "filter bubbles" that effectively prevent them from encountering information that challenges their biases or assumptions.[18] Extensive profiles about individuals and their preferences are being painstakingly developed by companies that acquire and process increasing amounts of data. Public awareness of the scope and scale of these activities is limited, however, and consumers have few opportunities to control the collection, use, and re-use of these data profiles.

De-identification and re-identification

As techniques like data fusion make big data analytics more powerful, the challenges to current expectations of privacy grow more serious. When data is initially linked to an individual or device, some privacy-protective technology seeks to remove this linkage, or "de-identify" personally identifiable information—but equally effective techniques exist to pull the pieces back together through "re-identification." Similarly, integrating diverse data can lead to what some analysts call the "mosaic effect," whereby personally identifiable information can be derived or inferred from datasets that do not even include personal identifiers, bringing into focus a picture of who an individual is and what he or she likes.

Many technologists are of the view that de-identification of data as a means of protecting individual privacy is, at best, a limited proposition.[19] In practice, data collected and de-identified is protected in this form by companies' commitments to not re-identify the data and by security measures put in place to ensure those protections. Encrypting data, removing unique identifiers, perturbing data so it no longer identifies individuals, or giving users more say over how their data is used through personal profiles or controls are some of the current technological solutions. But meaningful de-identification may strip the data of both its usefulness and the ability to ensure its provenance and accountability. Moreover, it is difficult to predict how technologies to re-identify seemingly anonymized data may evolve. This creates substantial uncertainty about how an individual controls his or her own information and identity, and how he or she disputes decision-making based on data derived from multiple datasets.

The persistence of data

In the past, retaining physical control over one's personal information was often sufficient to ensure privacy. Documents could be destroyed, conversations forgotten, and records

---

[18] Cynthia Dwork and Deirdre Mulligan, "It's Not Privacy, and It's Not Fair," 66 *Stan. L. Rev. Online* 35 (2013).
[19] See PCAST report, *Big Data and Privacy*; Harvard Law Petrie-Flom Center, *Online Symposium on the Law, Ethics & Science of Re-identification Demonstrations*, http://blogs.law.harvard.edu/billofhealth/2013/05/13/online-symposium-on-the-law-ethics-science-of-re-identification-demonstrations/.

expunged. But in the digital world, information can be captured, copied, shared, and transferred at high fidelity and retained indefinitely. Volumes of data that were once unthinkably expensive to preserve are now easy and affordable to store on a chip the size of a grain of rice. As a consequence, data, once created, is in many cases effectively permanent. Furthermore, digital data often concerns multiple people, making personal control impractical. For example, who owns a photo—the photographer, the people represented in the image, the person who first posted it, or the site to which it was posted? The spread of these new technologies are fundamentally changing the relationship between a person and the data about him or her.

Certainly data is freely shared and duplicated more than ever before. The specific responsibilities of individuals, government, corporations, and the network of friends, partners, and other third parties who may come into possession of personal data have yet to be worked out. The technological trajectory, however, is clear: more and more data will be generated about individuals and will persist under the control of others. Ensuring that data is secure is a matter of the utmost importance. For that reason, models for public-private cooperation, like the Administration's Cybersecurity Framework, launched in February 2014, are a critical part of ensuring the security and resiliency of the critical infrastructure supporting much of the world's data assets.[20]

Affirming our Values

No matter how serious and consequential the questions posed by big data, this Administration remains committed to supporting the digital economy and the free flow of data that drives its innovation. The march of technology always raises questions about how to adapt our privacy and social values in response. The United States has met this challenge through considered debate in the public sphere, in the halls of Congress, and in the courts—and throughout its history has consistently been able to realize the rights enshrined in the Constitution, even as technology changes.

Since the earliest days of President Obama's first term, this Administration has called on both the public and private sector to harness the power of data in ways that boost productivity, improve lives, and serve communities. That said, this study is about more than the capabilities of big data technologies. It is also about how big data may challenge fundamental American values and existing legal frameworks. This report focuses on the federal government's role in assuring that our values endure and our laws evolve as big data technologies change the landscape for consumers and citizens.

In the last year, the public debate on privacy has largely focused on how government, particularly the intelligence community, collects, stores, and uses data. This report largely leaves issues raised by the use of big data in signals intelligence to be addressed through the policy guidance that the President announced in January. However, this re-

---

[20] President Barack Obama, *International Strategy for Cyberspace*, The White House, May 2011, http://www.whitehouse.gov/the-press-office/2014/02/12/launch-cybersecurity-framework.

port considers many of the other ways government collects and uses large datasets for the public good. Public trust is required for the proper functioning of government, and governments must be held to a higher standard for the collection and use of personal data than private actors. As President Obama has unequivocally stated, "It is not enough for leaders to say: trust us, we won't abuse the data we collect."[21]

Recognizing that big data technologies are used far beyond the intelligence community, this report has taken a broad view of the issues implicated by big data. These new technologies do not only test individual privacy, whether defined as the right to be let alone, the right to control one's identity, or some other variation. Some of the most profound challenges revealed during this review concern how big data analytics may lead to disparate inequitable treatment, particularly of disadvantaged groups, or create such an opaque decision-making environment that individual autonomy is lost in an impenetrable set of algorithms.

These are not unsolvable problems, but they merit deep and serious consideration. The historian Melvin Kranzberg's First Law of Technology is important to keep in mind: "Technology is neither good nor bad; nor is it neutral."[22] Technology can be used for the public good, but so too can it be used for individual harm. Regardless of technological advances, the American public retains the power to structure the policies and laws that govern the use of new technologies in a way that protects foundational values.

Big data is changing the world. But it is not changing Americans' belief in the value of protecting personal privacy, of ensuring fairness, or of preventing discrimination. This report aims to encourage the use of data to advance social good, particularly where markets and existing institutions do not otherwise support such progress, while at the same time supporting frameworks, structures, and research that help protect our core values.

---

[21] President Barack Obama, Remarks on the Administration's Review of Signals Intelligence, January 17, 2014, http://www.whitehouse.gov/the-press-office/2014/01/17/remarks-president-review-signals-intelligence.
[22] Melvin Kranzberg, "Technology and History: Kranzberg's Laws," 27.3 *Technology and Culture*, (1986) p. 544-560.

II. The Obama Administration's Approach to Open Data and Privacy

Throughout American history, technology and privacy laws have evolved in tandem. The United States has long been a leader in protecting individual privacy while supporting an environment of innovation and economic prosperity.

The Fourth Amendment to the Constitution protects the "right of the people to be secure in their persons, houses, papers, and effects, against unreasonable searches and seizures." Flowing from this protection of physical spaces and tangible assets is a broader sense of respect for security and dignity that is indispensable both to personal well-being and to the functioning of democratic society.[23] A legal framework for the protection of privacy interests has grown up in the United States that includes constitutional, federal, state, and common law elements. "Privacy" is thus not a narrow concept, but instead addresses a range of concerns reflecting different types of intrusion into a person's sense of self, each requiring different protections.

Data collection—and the use of data to serve the public good—has an equally long history in the United States. Article I, Section 2 of the Constitution mandates a decennial Census in order to apportion the House of Representatives. In practice, the Census has never been conducted as just a simple head count, but has always been used to determine more specific demographic information for public purposes.[24]

Since President Obama took office, the federal government has taken unprecedented steps to make more of its own data available to citizens, companies, and innovators. Since 2009, the Obama Administration has made tens of thousands of datasets public, hosting many of them on Data.gov, the central clearinghouse for U.S. government data. Treating government data as an asset and making it available, discoverable, and usable—in a word, open—strengthens democracy, drives economic opportunity, and improves citizens' quality of life.

---

[23] See, e.g., *City of Ontario v. Quon*, 560 U.S. 746, 755-56 (2010) ("The [Fourth] Amendment guarantees the privacy, dignity, and security of persons against certain arbitrary and invasive acts by officers of the Government."); *Kyllo v. United States*, 533 U.S. 27, 31 (2001) ("'At the very core' of the Fourth Amendment 'stands the right of a man to retreat into his own home and there be free from unreasonable governmental intrusion.'"); *Olmstead v. United States*, 277 U.S. 438, 478 (1928) (Brandeis, J., dissenting) ("They [the Framers] sought to protect Americans in their beliefs, their thoughts, their emotions and their sensations. They conferred, as against the Government, the right to be let alone—the most comprehensive of rights and the right most valued by civilized men.").

[24] For example, e.g. the 1790 Census counted white men "over 16" and "under 16" separately to determine military eligibility. United States Census Bureau, "History," https://www.census.gov/history/www/through_the_decades/index_of_questions/1790_1.html; Margo Anderson, *The American Census: A Social History*, (Yale University Press, 1988).

Deriving value from open data requires developing the tools to understand and analyze it. So the Obama Administration has also made significant investments in the basic science of data analytics, storage, encryption, cybersecurity, and computing power.

The Obama Administration has made these investments while also recognizing that the collection, use, and sharing of data pose serious challenges. Federal research dollars have supported work to address the technological and ethical issues that arise when handling large-scale data sets. Drawing on the United States' long history of leadership on privacy issues, the Obama Administration also issued a groundbreaking consumer privacy blueprint in 2012 that included a Consumer Privacy Bill of Rights.[25] In 2014, the President announced the Cybersecurity Framework, developed in partnership with the private sector, to strengthen the security of the nation's critical infrastructure.[26]

This chapter charts the intersections of these initiatives—ongoing efforts to harness data for the public good while ensuring the rights of citizens and consumers are protected.

Open Data in the Obama Administration

Open Data Initiatives

The smartphones we carry around in our pockets tell us where we are by drawing on open government data. Decades ago, the federal government first made meteorological data and the Global Positioning System freely available, enabling entrepreneurs to create a wide range of new tools and services, from weather apps to automobile navigation systems.

In the past, data collected by the government mostly stayed in the government agency that collected it. The Obama Administration has launched a series of Open Data Initiatives, each unleashing troves of valuable data that were previously hard to access, in domains including health, energy, climate, education, public safety, finance, and global development. Executive Order 13642, signed by President Obama on May 9, 2013, established an important new principle in federal stewardship of data: going forward, agencies must consider openness and machine-readability as the new defaults for government information, while appropriately safeguarding privacy, confidentiality, and security.[27] Extending these open data efforts is also a core element of the President's Second Term Management Agenda, and the Office of Management and Budget has directed

---

[25] President Barack Obama, *Consumer Data Privacy In A Networked World: A Framework For Protecting Privacy And Promoting Innovation In The Global Digital Economy*, The White House, February 2012, http://www.whitehouse.gov/sites/default/files/privacy-final.pdf.

[26] National Institute of Standards & Technology, *Framework for Improving Critical Infrastructure Cybersecurity*, February 12, 2014, http://www.nist.gov/cyberframework/upload/cybersecurity-framework-021214-final.pdf.

[27] President Barack Obama, Making Open and Machine Readable the New Default for Government Information, Executive Order 13642, May 2013, http://www.whitehouse.gov/the-press-office/2013/05/09/executive-order-making-open-and-machine-readable-new-default-government.

agencies to release more of the administrative information they use to make decisions so it might be useful to others.[28]

At Data.gov the public can find everything from data regarding complaints made to the federal Consumer Financial Protection Bureau about private student loans to 911 service area boundaries for the state of Arkansas. The idea is that anyone can use Data.gov to find the open data they are looking for without having specialized knowledge of government agencies or programs within those agencies. Interested software developers can use simple tools to automatically access the datasets.

Federal agencies must also prioritize their data release efforts in part based on requests from the public. Each agency is required to solicit input through digital feedback mechanisms, like an email address or an online platform. For the first time, any advocate, entrepreneur, or researcher can connect with the federal government and suggest what data should be made available. To further improve feedback and encourage productive use of open government data, Administration officials have hosted and participated in a range of code-a-thons, brainstorming workshops ("Data Jams"), showcase events ("Datapaloozas"), and other meetings about open government data.[29]

Pursuant to the May 2013 Executive Order, the Office of Management and Budget and the Office of Science and Technology Policy released a framework for agencies to manage information as an asset throughout its lifecycle, which includes requirements to continue to protect personal, sensitive, and confidential data.[30] Agencies already categorize data assets into three access levels—public, restricted public, and non-public—and publish only the public catalog. To promote transparency, agencies include information in their external data inventories about technically public data assets that have not yet been posted online.

My Data Initiatives

Making public government data more open and machine-readable is only one element of the Administration's approach to data. The Privacy Act of 1974 grants citizens certain rights of access to their personal information. That access should be easy, secure, and useful. Starting in 2010, the Obama Administration launched a series of My Data initiatives to empower Americans with secure access to their personal data and increase citi-

---

[28] Office of Management and Budget, Guidance for Providing and Using Administrative Data for Statistical Purposes, (OMB M-144-06), February 14, 2014, http://www.whitehouse.gov/sites/default/files/omb/memoranda/2014/m-14-06.pdf.

[29] These events have helped federal agencies showcase government data resources being made freely available; collaborate with innovators about how open government data can be used to fuel new products, services, and companies; launch new challenges and incentive prizes designed to spur innovative use of data; and highlight how new uses of open government data are making a tangible impact in American lives and advancing the national interest.

[30] Specifically, the Open Data Policy (OMB M-13-13) requires agencies to collect or create information in a way that supports downstream information processing and dissemination; to maintain internal and external data asset inventories; and to clarify information management responsibilities. Agencies must also use machine-readable and open formats, data standards, and common core and extensible metadata.

zens' access to private-sector applications and services that can be used to analyze it. The My Data initiatives include:

- **Blue Button:** The Blue Button allows consumers to securely access their health information so they can better manage their health care and finances and share their information with providers. In 2010, the U.S. Department of Veterans Affairs launched the Blue Button to give veterans the ability to download their health records. Since then, more than 5.4 million veterans have used the Blue Button tool to access their personal health information. More than 500 companies in the private sector have pledged their support to increase patient access to their health data by leveraging Blue Button, and today, more than 150 million Americans have the promise of being able to access their digital health information from health care providers, medical laboratories, retail pharmacy chains, and state immunization registries.

- **Get Transcript:** In 2014, the Internal Revenue Service made it possible for taxpayers to digitally access their last three years of tax information through a tool called Get Transcript. Individual taxpayers can use Get Transcript to download a record of past tax returns, which makes it easier to apply for mortgages, student loans, and business loans, or to prepare future tax filings.

- **Green Button:** The Administration partnered with electric utilities in 2012 to create the Green Button, which provides families and business with easy access to their energy usage information in a consumer-friendly and computer-friendly format. Today, 48 utilities and electricity suppliers serving more than 59 million homes and businesses have committed to giving their customers "Green Button" access to help them save energy. With customers in control of their energy data, they can choose which private sector tools and services can help them better manage their property's energy efficiency.[31]

- **MyStudentData:** The Department of Education makes it possible for students and borrowers to access and download their data from the Free Application for Federal Student Aid and their federal student loan information—including loan, grant, enrollment, and overpayment information. In both cases, the information is available via a user-friendly, machine-readable, plain-text file.

Beyond providing people with easy and secure access to their data, the My Data initiatives helps establish a strong model for personal data accessibility that the Administration hopes will become widely adopted in the private and public sectors. The ability to access one's personal information will be increasingly important in the future, when more aspects of life will involve data transactions between individuals, companies, and institutions.

---

[31] Aneesh Chopra, "Green Button: Providing Consumers with Access to Their Energy Data," *Office of Science and Technology Policy Blog*, January 2012, http://www.whitehouse.gov/blog/2012/01/18/green-button-providing-consumers-access-their-energy-data.

Big Data Initiative: "Data to Knowledge to Action"

At its core, big data is about being able to move quickly from data to knowledge to action. On March 29, 2012, six federal agencies joined forces to launch the "Big Data Research and Development Initiative," with over $200 million in research funding to improve the tools and techniques needed to access, organize, and glean discoveries from huge volumes of digital data.

Since the launch of this "Data to Knowledge to Action" initiative, DARPA has created an "Open Catalog" of the research publications and open source software generated by its $100 million XDATA program, an effort to process and analyze large sets of imperfect, incomplete data.[32] The National Institutes of Health has supported a $50 million "Big Data to Knowledge" program about biomedical big data. The National Science Foundation has funded big data research projects which have reduced the cost of processing a human genome by a factor of 40. The Department of Energy announced a $25 million Scalable Data Management, Analysis, and Visualization Institute, which produced climate data techniques that have made seasonal hurricane predictions more than 25 percent more accurate. Many other research initiatives have important big data components, including the BRAIN Initiative, announced by President Obama in April 2013. As part of the Administration's big data research initiative, the National Science Foundation has also funded specific projects examining the social, ethical, and policy aspects of big data.

U.S. Privacy Law and International Privacy Frameworks

Development of Privacy Law in the United States

U.S. privacy laws have shaped and been shaped by societal changes, including the waves of technological innovation set in motion by the industrial revolution. The first portable cameras helped catalyze Samuel Warren and Louis Brandeis's seminal 1890 article *The Right to Privacy*, in which they note that "[r]ecent inventions and business methods call attention to the next step which must be taken for the protection of the person, and for securing to the individual ... the right 'to be let alone'... numerous mechanical devices threaten to make good the prediction that 'what is whispered in the closet shall be proclaimed from the house-tops.'"[33] This prescient work laid the foundation for the common law of privacy in the 20th century, establishing citizens' rights to privacy from the government and from each other.[34]

---

[32] In November 2013, the White House organized a "Data to Knowledge to Action" event that featured dozens of announcements of new public, private, academic and non-profit initiatives. From transforming how research universities prepare students to become data scientists to allowing more citizens and entrepreneurs to access and analyze the huge amounts of space-based data that NASA collects about the Earth, the commitments promise to spur tremendous progress. The Administration is also working to increase the number of data scientists who are actively engaged in solving hard problems in education, health care, sustainability, informed decision-making, and non-profit effectiveness.

[33] Samuel Warren and Louis Brandeis, "The Right to Privacy," 4 *Harvard Law Review* 193, 195 (1890).

[34] See William Prosser, "Privacy," 48 *California Law Review* 383 (1960).

Over the course of the last century, case law about what constitutes a "search" for purposes of the Fourth Amendment to the Constitution has developed with time and technology.[35] In 1928, the U.S. Supreme Court held in *Olmstead v. United States* that placing wiretaps on a phone line located outside of a person's house did not violate the Fourth Amendment, even though the government obtained the content from discussions *inside* the home.[36] But the *Olmstead* decision was arguably more famous for the dissent written by Justice Brandeis, who wrote that the Founders had "conferred, as against the government, the right to be let alone—the most comprehensive of rights and the right most favored by civilized men."[37]

The Court's opinion in *Olmstead* remained the law of the land until it was overturned by the Court's 1967 decision in *Katz v. United States*. In *Katz*, the Court held that the FBI's placement of a recording device on the outside of a public telephone booth without a warrant qualified as a search that violated the "reasonable expectation of privacy" of the person using the booth, even though the device did not physically penetrate the booth, his person, or his property. Under *Katz*, an individual's subjective expectations of privacy are protected when society regards them as reasonable.[38]

Civil courts did not immediately acknowledge privacy as justification for one citizen to bring a lawsuit against another—what lawyers call a "cause of action." It wasn't until the 1934 Restatement (First) of Torts that an "unreasonable and serious" invasion of privacy was recognized as a basis to sue.[39] Courts in most states began to recognize privacy as a cause of action, although what emerged from decisions was not a single tort, but instead "a complex of four" potential torts:[40]

1. Intrusion upon a person's seclusion or solitude, or into his private affairs.
2. Public disclosure of embarrassing private facts about an individual.
3. Publicity placing one in a false light in the public eye.
4. Appropriation of one's likeness for the advantage of another.[41]

Some contemporary critics argue the "complex of four" does not sufficiently recognize privacy issues that arise from the extensive collection, use, and disclosure of personal information by businesses in the modern marketplace. Others suggest that automated

---

[35] Wayne Lafave, "Search and Seizure: A Treatise On The Fourth Amendment," §§ 1.1–1.2 (West Publishing, 5th ed. 2011).

[36] *Olmstead v. United States,* 277 U.S. 438 (1928).

[37] Ibid at 478.

[38] *Katz v. United States*, 389 U.S. 347, 361 (1967) (Harlan, J., concurring); see also LaFave, supra note 35 § 2.1(b) ("[L]ower courts attempting to interpret and apply Katz quickly came to rely upon the Harlan elaboration, as ultimately did a majority of the Supreme Court.").

[39] Restatement (First) Torts § 867 (1939).

[40] Prosser, supra note 34 at 389 (1960).

[41] Ibid. See also Restatement (Second) Torts § 652A (1977) (Prosser's privacy torts incorporated into the Restatement).

processing should in fact ease privacy concerns because it uses computers operated under precise controls to perform tasks that used to be handled by a person.[42]

The Fair Information Practice Principles

As computing advanced and became more widely used by government and the private sector, policymakers around the world began to tackle the issue of privacy anew. In 1973, the U.S. Department of Health, Education, and Welfare issued a report entitled *Records, Computers, and the Rights of Citizens*.[43] The report analyzed "harmful consequences that might result from automated personal data systems" and recommended certain safeguards for the use of information. Those safeguards, commonly known today as the "Fair Information Practice Principles," or "FIPPs," form the bedrock of modern data protection regimes.

While the principles are instantiated in law and international agreements in different ways, at their core, the FIPPs articulate basic protections for handling personal data. They provide that an individual has a right to know what data is collected about him or her and how it is used. The individual should further have a right to object to some uses and to correct inaccurate information. The organization that collects information has an obligation to ensure that the data is reliable and kept secure. These principles, in turn, served as the basis for the Privacy Act of 1974, which regulates the federal government's maintenance, collection, use, and dissemination of personal information in systems of records.[44]

By the late 1970s, several other countries had also passed national privacy laws.[45] In 1980, the Organization for Economic Cooperation and Development (OECD) issued its "Guidelines Governing the Protection of Privacy and Transborder Flow of Personal Data."[46] Building on the FIPPs, the OECD guidelines have informed national privacy laws, sector-specific laws, and best practices for the past three decades. In 1981, the Council of Europe also completed work on the Convention for the Protection of Individuals with regard to Automatic Processing of Personal Data (Convention 108), which applied a FIPPs approach to emerging privacy concerns in Europe.

Despite some important differences, the privacy frameworks in the United States and those countries following the EU model are both based on the FIPPs. The European approach, which is based on a view that privacy is a fundamental human right, generally involves top-down regulation and the imposition of across-the-board rules restricting the use of data or requiring explicit consent for that use. The United States, in contrast, em-

---

[42] Ibid.

[43] See, e.g., K.A. Taipale, "Data Mining and Domestic Security: Connecting the Dots to Make Sense of Data," V *The Columbia Science and Technology Review*, (2003), http://papers.ssrn.com/sol3/papers.cfm?abstract_id=546782.

[44] Pub. L. 93-579 (codified at 5 U.S.C. § 552a).

[45] Organization for Economic Cooperation and Development, *Thirty Years After The OECD Privacy Guidelines*, 2011, p. 17, http://www.oecd.org/sti/ieconomy/49710223.pdf.

[46] Ibid at 27.

ploys a sectoral approach that focuses on regulating specific risks of privacy harm in particular contexts, such as health care and credit. This places fewer broad rules on the use of data, allowing industry to be more innovative in its products and services, while also sometimes leaving unregulated potential uses of information that fall between sectors.

The FIPPs form a common thread through these sectoral laws and a variety of international agreements. They are woven into the 2004 Asia Pacific Economic Cooperation Privacy Principles, which was endorsed by APEC economies, and form the basis for the U.S.-E.U. and U.S.-Switzerland Safe Harbor Frameworks, which harness the global consensus around the FIPPs as a means to build bridges between U.S. and European law. [47]

Sector-Specific Privacy Laws in the United States

In the United States during the 1970s and 80s, narrowly-tailored sectoral privacy laws began to supplement the tort-based body of common law. These sector-specific laws create privacy safeguards that apply only to specific types of entities and data. With a few exceptions, individual states and the federal government have predominantly enacted privacy laws on a sectoral basis.[48]

The Fair Credit Reporting Act (FCRA) was originally enacted in 1970 to promote accuracy, fairness, and privacy protection with regard to the information assembled by consumer reporting agencies for use in credit and insurance reports, employee background checks, and tenant screenings. The law protects consumers by providing specific rights to access and correct their information. It requires companies that prepare consumer reports to ensure data is accurate and complete; limits when such reports may be used; and requires agencies to provide notice when an adverse action, such as the denial of credit, is taken based on the content of a report.

The 1996 Health Insurance Portability and Accountability Act (HIPAA) addresses the use and disclosure of individuals' health information by specified "covered entities" and includes standards designed to help individuals understand and control how their health information is used.[49] A key aspect of HIPAA is the principle of "minimum necessary"

---

[47] The APEC Privacy Principles are associated with the 2004 APEC Privacy Framework and APEC Cross Border Privacy Rules system approved in 2011. See Asia-Pacific Economic Cooperation, "APEC Privacy Principles," 2005, p. 3, http://www.apec.org/Groups/Committee-on-Trade-and-Investment/~/media/Files/Groups/ECSG/05_ecsg_privacyframewk.ashx; *Consumer Data Privacy In A Networked World*, p 49-52; export.gov/safeharbor for information on the U.S.-EU and U.S.-Swiss Safe Harbor Frameworks. These enforceable self-certification programs are administered by the U.S. Department of Commerce and were developed in consultation with the European Commission and the Federal Data Protection and Information Commissioner of Switzerland, respectively, to provide a streamlined means for U.S. organizations to comply with EU and Swiss data protection laws.

[48] California, for example, has a right to privacy in the state Constitution. Cal. Const. art. 1 § 1.

[49] See U.S. Department of Health and Human Services, Health Information Privacy, "Summary of the HIPAA Privacy Rule," http://www.hhs.gov/ocr/privacy/hipaa/understanding/summary/index.html

use and disclosure.[50] Congress and the Department of Health and Human Services have periodically updated protections for personal health data. The Children's Online Privacy Protection Act of 1998 (COPPA) and the Federal Trade Commission's implementing regulations require online services directed at children under the age of 13, or which collect personal data from children, to obtain verifiable parental consent to do so. In the financial sector, the Gramm-Leach-Bliley Act mandates that financial institutions respect the privacy of customers and the security and confidentiality of those customers' nonpublic personal information. Other sectoral privacy laws safeguard individuals' educational, communications, video rental, and genetic information.[51]

Consumer Privacy Bill of Rights

In February 2012, the White House released a report titled *Consumer Data Privacy in a Networked World: A Framework for Protecting Privacy and Promoting Innovation in the Global Digital Economy.*[52] This "Privacy Blueprint" contains four key elements: a Consumer Privacy Bill of Rights based on the Fair Information Practice Principles; a call for government-convened multi-stakeholder processes to apply those principles in particular business contexts; support for effective enforcement of privacy rights, including the enactment of baseline consumer privacy legislation; and a commitment to international privacy regimes that support the flow of data across borders.

At the center of the Privacy Blueprint is the Consumer Privacy Bill of Rights, which states clear baseline protections for consumers. The rights are:

- **Individual Control:** Consumers have a right to exercise control over what personal data organizations collect from them and how they use it.

- **Transparency:** Consumers have a right to easily understandable information about privacy and security practices.

- **Respect for Context:** Consumers have a right to expect that organizations will collect, use, and disclose personal data in ways that are consistent with the context in which consumers provide the data.

- **Security:** Consumers have a right to secure and responsible handling of personal data.

- **Access and Accuracy:** Consumers have a right to access and correct personal data in usable formats, in a manner that is appropriate to the sensitivity of the data and the risk of adverse consequences to consumers if the data are inaccurate.

---

[50] This principle ensures that covered entities make reasonable efforts to use, disclose, and request only the minimum amount of protected health information needed to accomplish the intended purpose of the use, disclosure, or request. See U.S. Department of Health & Human Services, Health Information Privacy, "Minimum Necessary Requirement,"
http://www.hhs.gov/ocr/privacy/hipaa/understanding/coveredentities/minimumnecessary.html.
[51] They include: The Fair Credit Reporting Act of 1970, the Family Educational Rights and Privacy Act of 1974, the Electronic Communications Privacy Act of 1986, the Computer Fraud and Abuse Act of 1986, the Cable Communications Policy Act of 1984, the Video Privacy Protection Act of 1998, and the Genetic Information Nondiscrimination Act of 2008.
[52] See *Consumer Data Privacy In A Networked World, p 25.*

- **Focused Collection:** Consumers have a right to reasonable limits on the personal data that companies collect and retain.

- **Accountability:** Consumers have a right to have personal data handled by companies with appropriate measures in place to assure they adhere to the Consumer Privacy Bill of Rights.

The Consumer Privacy Bill of Rights is more focused on consumers than previous privacy frameworks, which were often couched in legal jargon. For example, it describes a right to "access and accuracy," which is more easily understood by users than previous formulations referencing "data quality and integrity." Similarly, it assures consumers that companies will respect the "context" in which data is collected and used, replacing the term "purpose specification."

The Consumer Privacy Bill of Rights also draws upon the Fair Information Practice Principles to better accommodate the online environment in which we all now live. Instead of requiring companies to adhere to a single, rigid set of requirements, the Consumer Privacy Bill of Rights establishes general principles that afford companies discretion in how they implement them. The Consumer Privacy Bill of Rights' "context" principle interacts with its other six principles, assuring consumers that their data will be collected and used in ways consistent with their expectations. At the same time, the context principle permits companies to develop new services using personal information when that use is consistent with the companies' relationship with its users and the circumstances surrounding how it collects data.

The Internet's complexity, global reach, and constant evolution require timely, scalable, and innovation-enabling policies. To answer this challenge, the Privacy Blueprint calls for all relevant stakeholders to come together to develop voluntary, enforceable codes of conduct that specify how the Consumer Privacy Bill of Rights applies in specific business contexts. The theory behind the Consumer Privacy Bill of Rights is that this combination of broad baseline principles and specific codes of conduct can protect consumers while supporting innovation.

Promoting Global Interoperability

The Obama Administration released the Consumer Privacy Bill of Rights as other countries and international organizations began to review their own privacy frameworks. In 2013, the OECD updated its Privacy Guidelines, which supplement the Fair Information Practice Principles with mechanisms to implement and enforce privacy protections. The APEC Cross Border Privacy Rules System, also announced in 2013, largely follows the OECD guidelines.[53] The Council of Europe is undertaking a review of Convention 108. Building bridges among these different privacy frameworks is critical to ensuring robust international commerce.

---

[53] Organization for Economic Cooperation and Development, "OECD Work on Privacy," http://www.oecd.org/sti/ieconomy/privacy.htm.

The European Union is also in the process of reforming its data protection rules.[54] The current E.U. Data Protection Directive only allows transfers of E.U. citizens' data to those non-E.U. countries with "adequate" privacy laws or mechanisms providing sufficient safeguards for data, such as the U.S.-E.U. Safe Harbor. In January 2014, the U.S. and E.U. began discussing how best to enhance the Safe Harbor Framework to ensure that it continues to provide strong data protection and enable trade through increased transparency, effective enforcement, and legal certainty. These negotiations continue, even as Europe—like the United States—wrestles with questions about how it will accommodate big data technologies and increased computational and storage capacities.[55]

In March 2014, the Federal Trade Commission, together with agency officials from the European Union and Asia-Pacific Economic Cooperation economies, announced joint E.U. and APEC endorsement of a document that maps the requirements of the European and APEC privacy frameworks.[56] The mapping project will help companies seeking certification to do business in both E.U. and APEC countries recognize overlaps and gaps between the two frameworks.[57] Efforts like these clarify obligations for companies and help build interoperability between global privacy frameworks.

Conclusion

The most common privacy risks today still involve "small data"—the targeted compromise of, for instance, personal banking information for purposes of financial fraud. These risks do not involve especially large volumes, rapid velocities, or great varieties of information, nor do they implicate the kind of sophisticated analytics associated with big data. Protecting privacy of "small" data has been effectively addressed in the United States through the Fair Information Practice Principles, sector-specific laws, robust enforcement, and global privacy assurance mechanisms.

Privacy scholars, policymakers, and technologists are now turning to the question of how big data technology can be effectively managed under the FIPPs-based frameworks. The remainder of this report explores applications of big data in the public and private sector and then returns to consider the overall implications big data may have on current privacy frameworks.

---

[54] European Commission, "Commission Proposes a Comprehensive Reform of the Data Protection Rules," January 25, 2012, http://ec.europa.eu/justice/newsroom/data-protection/news/120125_en.htm.

[55] See Joined Cases C-293/12 and C-594/12, Digital Rights Ireland Ltd. v. Minister for Communications, Marine and Natural Resources, et al. (Apr. 8, 2014) in which the European Court of Justice invalidated the data retention requirements applied to electronic communications on the basis that the scope of the requirements interfered in a "particularly serious manner with the fundamental rights to respect for private life and to the protection of personal data."

[56] European Commission, Article 29 Data Protection Working Party, Press Release: "Promoting Cooperation on Data Transfer Systems Between Europe and the Asia-Pacific," March 26, 2013, http://ec.europa.eu/justice/data-protection/article-29/press-material/press-release/art29_press_material/20130326_pr_apec_en.pdf.

[57] Article 29 Data Protection Working Party, Opinion 02/2014 on a referential for requirements for Binding Corporate Rules, February 27, 2014, http://ec.europa.eu/justice/data-protection/article-29/documentation/opinion-recommendation/files/2014/wp212_en.pdf.

III. Public Sector Management of Data

Government keeps the peace. It makes sure our food is safe to eat. It keeps our air and water clean. The laws and regulations it promulgates order economic and political life. Big data technology stands to improve nearly all the services the public sector delivers.

This chapter explores how big data is already helping the government carry out its obligations in health, education, homeland security, and law enforcement. It also begins to frame some of the challenges big data raises. Questions about what the government should and should not do, and how the rights of citizens should be protected in light of changing technology, are as old as the Republic itself. In framing the laws and norms of our young country, the founders took pains to demarcate private spheres shielded from inappropriate government interference. While many things about the big data world might astonish them, the founders would not be surprised to find that the Constitution and Bill of Rights are as central to the debate as Moore's law and zettabytes.

At its core, public-sector use of big data heightens concerns about the balance of power between government and the individual. Once information about citizens is compiled for a defined purpose, the temptation to use it for other purposes can be considerable, especially in times of national emergency. One of the most shameful instances of the government misusing its own data dates to the Second World War. Census data collected under strict guarantees of confidentiality was used to identify neighborhoods where Japanese-Americans lived so they could be detained in internment camps for the duration of the war.

Because the government bears a special responsibility to protect its citizens when exercising power and authority for the public good, how big data should be put to use in the public sector, as well as what controls and limitations should apply, must be carefully considered. If unchecked, big data could be a tool that substantially expands government power over citizens. At the same time, big data can also be used to enhance accountability and to engineer systems that are inherently more respectful of privacy and civil rights.

Big Data and Health Care Delivery

Data has long been a part of health care delivery. In the past several years, legislation has created incentives for health care providers to transition to using electronic health records, vastly expanding the volume of health data available to clinicians, researchers, and patients. With the enactment of the Affordable Care Act, the model for health care reimbursement is beginning to shift from paying for isolated and potentially uncoordinated instances of treatment—a model called "fee-for-service"—to paying on the basis of better health outcomes. Taken together, these trends are helping build a "learning" health care system where effective practices are identified from clinical data and then rapidly disseminated back to providers.

Big data can identify diet, exercise, preventive care, and other lifestyle factors that help keep people from having to seek care from a doctor. Big data analytics can also help identify clinical treatments, prescription drugs, and public health interventions that may not appear to be effective in smaller samples, across broad populations, or using traditional research methods. From a payment perspective, big data can be used to ensure professionals who treat patients have strong performance records and are reimbursed on the quality of patient outcomes rather than the quantity of care delivered.

The emerging practice of predictive medicine is the ultimate application of big data in health. This powerful technology peers deeply into a person's health status and genetic information, allowing doctors to better predict whether individuals will develop a disease and how they might respond to specific therapies. Predictive medicine raises many complex issues. Traditionally, health data privacy policies have sought to protect the identity of individuals whose information is being shared and analyzed. But increasingly, data about groups or categories of people will be used to identify diseases prior to or very early after the onset of clinical symptoms.

But the information that stands to be discovered by predictive medicine extends beyond a single individual's risks to include others with similar genes, potentially including the children and future descendants of those whose information is originally collected. Bio-repositories that link genomic data to health care data are on the leading edge of confronting important questions about personal privacy in the context of health research and treatment.[58]

The privacy frameworks that currently cover information now used in health may not be well suited to address these developments or facilitate the research that drives them. Using big data to improve health requires advanced analytical models to ingest multiple kinds of lifestyle, genomic, medical, and financial data. The powerful connection between lifestyle and health outcomes means the distinction between personal data and health care data has begun to blur. These types of data are subjected to different and sometimes conflicting federal and state regulation, including the Health Insurance Portability and Accountability Act, Gramm-Leach-Bliley Act, Fair Credit Reporting Act, and Federal Trade Commission Act. The complexity of complying with numerous laws when data is combined from various sources raises the potential need to carve out special data use authorities for the health care industry if it is to realize the potential health gains and cost reductions that could come from big data analytics. At the same time, health organizations interact with many organizations that are not regulated under any of these

---

[58] Bradley Malin and Latanya Sweeney, "How (not) to protect genomic data privacy in a distributed network: using trail re-identification to evaluate and design anonymity protection systems," *Journal of Biomedical Informatics* (2004), http://www.j-biomed-inform.com/article/S1532-0464(04)00053-X.

laws.[59] In the resulting ecosystem, personal health information of various kinds is shared with an array of firms, and even sold by state governments, in ways that might not accord with consumer expectations of the privacy of their medical data.

Though medicine is changing, information about our health remains a very private part of our lives. As big data enables ever more powerful discoveries, it will be important to revisit how privacy is protected as information circulates among all the partners involved in care. Health care leaders have voiced the need for a broader trust framework to grant all health information, regardless of its source, some level of privacy protection. This may potentially involve crafting additional protections beyond those afforded in the Health Insurance Portability and Accountability Act and Genetic Information Non-Discrimination Act as well as streamlining data interoperability and compliance requirements. After studying health information technology, the President's Council of Advisors on Science & Technology concluded that the nation needs to adopt universal standards and an architecture that will facilitate controlled access to information across many different types of records.[60]

Modernizing the health care data privacy framework will require careful negotiation between the many parties involved in delivering health care and insurance to Americans, but the potential economic and health benefits make it well worth the effort.

Learning about Learning: Big Data and Education

Education at both the K-12 and university levels is now supported inside and outside the classroom by a range of technologies that help foster and enhance the learning process. Students now access class materials, watch instructional videos, comment on class activities, collaborate with each other, complete homework, and take tests online.

Technology-based educational tools and platforms offer important new capabilities for students and teachers. After only a few generations of evolution, these tools provide real-time assessment so that material can be presented based on how quickly a student learns. Education technologies can also be scaled to reach broad audiences, enable continuous improvement of course content, and increase engagement among students.[61]

Beyond personalizing education, the availability of new types of data profoundly improves researchers' ability to learn about learning. Data from a student's experience in massive open online courses (MOOCs) or other technology-based learning platforms

---

[59] Latanya Sweeney, a Professor of Government and Technology in Residence at Harvard University, has studied information flows in the health care industry. A graphical map of data flows that depicts information flows outside entities regulated by HIPAA can be found at www.thedatamap.org.

[60] President's Council of Advisors on Science & Technology, *Realizing the Full Potential Of Health Information Technology to Improve Health Care for Americans: The Path Forward*, The White House, December 2010, http://www.whitehouse.gov/sites/default/files/microsites/ostp/pcast-health-it-report.pdf.

[61] President's Council of Advisors on Science & Technology, *Harnessing Technology for Higher Education*, The White House, December 2013, http://www.whitehouse.gov/sites/default/files/microsites/ostp/PCAST/pcast_edit_dec-2013.pdf.

can be precisely tracked, opening the door to understanding how students move through a learning trajectory with greater fidelity, and at greater scale, than traditional education research is able to achieve. This includes gaining insight into student access of learning activities, measuring optimal practice periods for meeting different learning objectives, creating pathways through material for different learning approaches, and using that information to help students who are struggling in similar ways. Already, the Department of Education has studied how to harness these technologies, begun integrating the use of data from online education in the National Education Technology Plan, and laid plans for a Virtual Learning Lab to pioneer the methodological tools for this research.[62]

The big data revolution in education also raises serious questions about how best to protect student privacy as technology reaches further into the classroom. While states and local communities have traditionally played the dominant role in providing education, much of the software that supports online learning tools and courses is provided by for-profit firms. This raises complicated questions about who owns the data streams coming off online education platforms and how they can be used. Applying privacy safeguards like the Family Educational Rights and Privacy Act, the Protection of Pupil Rights Amendment, or the Children's Online Privacy Protection Act to educational records can create unique challenges.

Protecting Children's Privacy in the Era of Big Data

Children today are among the first generation to grow up playing with digital devices even before they learn to read. In the United States, children and teenagers are active users of mobile apps and social media platforms. As they use these technologies, granular data about them—some of it sensitive—is stored and processed online. This data has the potential to dramatically improve learning outcomes and open new opportunities for children, but could be used to build an invasive consumer profile of them once they become adults, or otherwise pose problems later in their lives. Although youth on average are typically no less, and in many cases more, cognizant of commercial and government use of data than adults, they often face scrutiny by parents, teachers, college admissions officers, military recruiters, and case workers. Vulnerable youth, including foster children and homeless youth, who typically have little adult guidance, are also particularly susceptible to data misuse and identity theft. Struggling to find some privacy in the face of tremendous supervision, many youth experiment with various ways to obscure the meaning of what they share except to select others, even if they are unable to limit access to the content itself.[63]

Because young people are exactly that—young—they need appropriate freedoms to explore and experiment safely and without the specter of being haunted by mistakes in the future. The Children's Online Privacy Protection Act requires website operators and app

---

[62] Department of Education, *Enhancing Teaching and Learning Through Educational Data Mining and Learning Analytics: An Issue Brief*, October 2012, http://www.ed.gov/edblogs/technology/files/2012/03/edm-la-brief.pdf. For information about the National Education technology plan, see www.tech.ed.gov/netp.
[63] danah boyd, *It's Complicated: The Social Lives of Networked Teens*, (Yale University Press, 2014), www.danah.org/books/ItsComplicated.pdf.

developers to gain consent from a parent or guardian before collecting personal information from children under the age of 13. There is not yet a settled understanding of what harms, if any, are accruing to children and what additional policy frameworks may be needed to ensure that growing up with technology will be an asset rather than a liability.

Just as with health care, some of the information revealed when a user interacts with a digital education platform can be very personal, including aptitude for particular types of learning and performance relative to other students. It is even possible to discern whether students have learning disabilities or have trouble concentrating for long periods. What time of day and for how long students stay signed in to online tools reveals lifestyle habits. What should educational institutions do with this data to improve learning opportunities for students? How can students who use these platforms, especially those in K-12 education, be confident that their data is safe?

To help answer complicated questions about ownership and proper usage of data, the U.S. Department of Education released guidance for online education services in February 2014.[64] This guidance makes clear that schools and districts can enter into agreements with third parties involving student data only so long as requirements under the Family Educational Rights and Privacy Act and Protection of Pupil Rights Amendment are met. As more online learning tools and services become available for kids, states and local governments are also watching these issues closely.[65] Schools and districts can only share protected student information to further legitimate educational interests, and they must retain "direct control" over that information. Even with this new guidance, the question of how best to protect student privacy in a big data world must be an ongoing conversation.

The Administration is committed to vigorously pursuing these questions and will work through the Department of Education so all students can experience the benefits of big data innovations in teaching and learning while being protected from potential harms.[66] As Secretary of Education Arne Duncan has said, "Student data must be secure, and treated as precious, no matter where it's stored. It is not a commodity."[67] This means en-

---

[64] Department of Education, *Protecting Student Privacy While Using Online Educational Services: Requirement and Best Practices*, February 2014,
http://ptac.ed.gov/sites/default/files/Student%20Privacy%20and%20Online%20Educational%20Services%20%28February%202014%29.pdf.

[65] For example, California recently passed a law prohibiting online services from gathering information about a minor's activities for marketing purposes, or from displaying certain online advertising to minors. The law further requires online services to delete information that the minor posted on the website or service, a right for which the statute has now been dubbed "the Eraser Law."

[66] The Department of Education is exploring data innovation and use in a wide variety of contexts, including making more educational data available through application programming interfaces. See David Soo, "How can the Department of Education Increase Innovation, Transparency and Access to Data?," *Department of Education Blog*, http://www.ed.gov/blog/2014/04/how-can-the-department-of-education-increase-innovation-transparency-and-access-to-data/.

[67] Department of Education, Technology in Education: Privacy and Progress, Remarks of U.S. Secretary of Education Arne Duncan at the Common Sense Media Privacy Zone Conference, February 24, 2014, https://www.ed.gov/news/speeches/technology-education-privacy-and-progress.

suring the personal information and online activity of students are protected from inappropriate uses, especially when it is gathered in an educational context.

Big Data at the Department of Homeland Security

Every day, two million passengers fly into, within, or over the United States. More than a million people enter the country by land. Verifying the identity of each person and determining whether he or she poses a threat falls to the Department of Homeland Security, which must process huge amounts of data in seconds to carry out its mission. The Department is not simply out to find the "needle in the haystack." Protecting the homeland often depends on finding the most critical needles across many haystacks—a classic big data problem.

Ensuring the Department efficiently and lawfully uses the information it collects is a massive undertaking. DHS was created out of 22 separate government agencies in the wake of the 9/11 attacks. Many of the databases DHS operates today are physically disconnected, run legacy operating systems, and are unable to integrate information across different security classifications. The Department also carries out a diverse portfolio of missions, each governed by separate authorities in law. At all times, information must be used only for authorized purposes and in ways that protect the privacy and civil liberties afforded to U.S. citizens and foreign nationals who enter or reside in the United States. Ensuring information is properly used falls to six offices at DHS headquarters.

Beginning in 2012, representatives of the Chief Information Officer, the policy division, and the intelligence division came together with privacy, civil liberties and legal oversight officers to begin developing the first department-wide big data capability, resident in two pilot programs named Neptune and Cerberus.[68] Neptune is designed from the ground up to be a "data lake" into which unclassified information from different sources flows.[69] It has multiple built-in safeguards, including the ability to apply multiple data tags and fine-grained rules to determine which users can access which data for what purpose. All of the data is tagged according to a precise scheme. The rules governing usage focus on whether there is an authorized purpose, mission, or "need to know," and whether the user has the appropriate job series and clearance to access the information. In this way, data tags can be combined with user attributes and context to govern what information is used where and by whom.

---

[68] Department of Homeland Security, *Privacy Impact Assessment for the Neptune Pilot*, September 2013, http://www.dhs.gov/sites/default/files/publications/privacy-pia-dhs-wide-neptune-09252013.pdf; "Privacy Impact Assessment for the Cerberus Pilot," November 22, 2013, http://www.dhs.gov/sites/default/files/publications/privacy-pia-dhs-cerberus-nov2013.pdf.

[69] In the first phase, three databases, from different parts of the agency, are fed into Neptune, where the data is then tagged and sorted. From there, the Department of Homeland Security feeds this tagged data into Cerberus, which operates at the classified level. Here, DHS can compare its unclassified and classified information.

A Model for Managing Data

To build the tagging standards that govern information in its big data pilots, the Department of Homeland Security brought together the owners of the data systems, called data stewards, with representatives from privacy, civil liberties, and legal oversight offices. For each database field, the group charted its attributes and how access to the data is granted to different user communities. After developing a set of tags to encode this information, they then considered what additional rules and protections were needed to account for specific use limitations or special cases governed by law or regulation. Tagging both enables precise access control and preserves links to source data and the purpose of its original collection. The end result is a taxonomy of rules governing where information goes and tracking where it came from and under what authority.

The fields in each database are grouped into three categories: core biographical data, such as name, date of birth, and citizenship status; extended biographical data, including addresses, phone number, and email; and detailed encounter data derived from electronic and in-person interactions with DHS. Encounter data is the most sensitive category. It may contain a law enforcement officer's observations about an individual they interview as well as allegations of a risk to homeland security they may pose. These data tags then allow precise rules to be set of who can access what information for what reason. In these two pilots, the majority of rules for negotiating access are consistent across DHS's different user communities. For example, many users will need access to the core biographic information of a particular data set to perform their missions. But some of the rules require far greater customization to account for specific use limitations.

The Neptune and Cerberus pilots also contain important controls around the types of searches that users are permitted to perform. A primary inspection agent may only need to perform a search on a specific person, because the agent is trying to confirm basic biographical information. However, an Immigration and Customs Investigator may need to perform person and characteristic searches while investigating a crime. DHS intelligence analysts may need to perform searches based on identities, characteristics, and trends when analyzing information related to a threat to homeland security. System administrators have no need to access the data contained within the system. The architecture of the database allows them to maintain the overall IT system but not to access any individual records.

The capabilities developed in these pilots are of a whole different order than the databases DHS inherited in 2002. Before these big data initiatives, it was not easy to perform searches across databases held by different components, let alone to aggregate them. In the past, users and system administrators might have been issued a login and username and granted total access, sometimes without an audit trail monitoring their use. Now, DHS will be able to more precisely grant access according to mission needs. Most importantly, by being deliberate in tagging and organizing the data in these advanced repositories, the agency can take on new kinds of predictive and anomaly analysis while complying with the law and subjecting its activities to robust oversight.

It's no accident that DHS was able to so carefully engineer how data is handled. DHS has both a dedicated Privacy Office and an Office for Civil Rights and Civil Liberties, each staffed with experts to help navigate this complex terrain.[70] Each pilot is accompanied by a detailed privacy impact assessment released to the public in advance of its operation. DHS has provided public briefings on the pilots and allowed members of the public to ask questions about the initiatives. The privacy and civil liberties oversight officials not only approved the plan for the pilots, they also approve tools or widgets built in the future to increase their functionality. All of this helps drive improvements to DHS's mission while ensuring that privacy and civil liberties concerns are considered from the start.

Upholding our Privacy Values in Law Enforcement

Big data can be a powerful tool for law enforcement. Recently, advanced web tools developed by DARPA's Memex program have helped federal law enforcement make substantial progress in identifying human trafficking networks in the United States. These tools comb the "surface web" we all know, as well as "deep web" pages that are also public but not indexed by commonly used search engines. By allowing searches across a wide range of websites, the tools uncover a wealth of information that might otherwise be difficult or time-intensive to obtain. Possible trafficking rings can be identified and cross-referenced with existing law enforcement databases, helping police officers map connections between sex trafficking and other illegal activity. Already, the tools have helped detect trafficking networks originating in Asia and spreading to several U.S. cities. It's a powerful example of how big data can help protect some of the most vulnerable people in the world.

Big data technologies provide effective tools to law enforcement and other agencies that protect our security, but they also pose difficult questions about their appropriate uses. Blending multiple data sources can create a fuller picture of a suspect's activities around the time of a crime, but can also aid in the creation of suspect profiles that focus scrutiny on particular individuals with little or no human intervention. Pattern analysis can reveal how criminal organizations are structured or can be used to make predictions about possible future crimes. Gathering broad datasets can help catch criminals, but can also sweep up detailed personal information about people who are not subjects of an investigation. When it comes to law enforcement, we must be careful to ensure that big data technologies are used in ways that take into account the needs to protect public safety and fairly enforce the laws, as well as the civil liberties and legitimate privacy interests of citizens.

Big data will naturally—and appropriately—be used differently in national security. A powerful intelligence system that harnesses global data to identify terrorist networks, to

---

[70] For more information, see the Department of Homeland Security's Privacy Office website, http://www.dhs.gov/privacy, and Office for Civil Rights and Civil Liberties, http://www.dhs.gov/office-civil-rights-and-civil-liberties.

provide warning of impending attacks, and to prevent the proliferation of weapons of mass destruction will operate under different legal authorities and oversight and have different privacy protections than a law enforcement system that helps allocate police resources to neighborhoods where higher levels of crime are predicted. Even though the applications are different, there are nevertheless important similarities in how privacy and civil rights are maintained across law enforcement and intelligence contexts. Privacy and legal officials must certify use of a system in each case, minimization rules are often employed to reduce information held, and data-tagging techniques are used to control access.

New Tools and New Challenges

The use of new technologies, especially in law enforcement, has given rise to important Constitutional jurisprudence.[71] As Justice Alito observed in a 2013 Supreme Court case concerning police placement of a GPS tracker on a suspect's car without a court order: "[I]t is almost impossible to think of late-18th-century situations that are analogous to what took place in this case. (Is it possible to imagine a case in which a constable secreted himself somewhere in a coach and remained there for a period of time in order to monitor the movements of the coach's owner?"[72] Alito noted further, "Something like this might have occurred in 1791, but this would have required either a gigantic coach, a very tiny constable, or both.)"[73]

The "tiny constable" has enormous implications. Ubiquitous surveillance—whether by GPS tracking, closed circuit TV, or virtually undetectable sensors—will increasingly figure in litigation about reasonable expectations of privacy and the proper uses and limits of law enforcement technology.

In recent decades, the cost of surveillance and the physical size of surveillance equipment have rapidly decreased. This has made it feasible for over 70 cities in the United States to install audio sensors that can pinpoint gunfire and rapidly dispatch police to a potential crime scene.[74] Given the speed of access and decreasing cost of storage, it has likewise become practical for even local police forces to actively collect and catalog data, like license plate and vehicle information, in real-time on a city-wide scale, and to also retain it for later use.[75]

The benefits of some of these technologies are tremendous. From finding missing persons to launching complex manhunts, the use of advanced surveillance technology by

---

[71] Most jurisprudence to date does not consider in their entirety big data technologies by the definition used in this report, but rather many of the advanced technologies, such as GPS trackers, that now play a crucial role in big data applications.

[72] *United States v. Jones*, 132 S.Ct. 945, 958 (2012) (Alito, J., concurring).

[73] Ibid at n.3.

[74] Over 70 cities in the U.S. use gunshot detection technology developed and provided by SST Solutions called ShotSpotter. For more information, please visit www.shotspotter.com.

[75] International Association of Chiefs of Police, *Privacy Impact Assessment Report for the Utilization of License Plate Readers*, September 2009, http://www.theiacp.org/Portals/0/pdfs/LPR_Privacy_Impact_Assessment.pdf.

federal, state, and local law enforcement can mean a faster and more effective response to criminal activity. It can also increase the chances that justice is reliably served in online crime, where criminals are among the earliest adopters of new technologies and law enforcement needs to have timely access to digital evidence.

Beyond surveillance, predictive technologies offer the potential for law enforcement to be better prepared to anticipate, intervene in, or outright prevent certain crimes. Some analytics software, such as one program in use by both the Los Angeles and Memphis police departments, employs predictive analytics to identify geographically-based "hotspots."[76] Many cities attribute meaningful declines in property crime to stepping up police patrols in "hotspot" areas.

Controversially, predictive analytics can now be applied to analyze a person's individual propensity to criminal activity.[77] In response to an epidemic of gang-related murders, the city of Chicago conducted a pilot that shifts the focus of predictive policing from geographical factors to identity. By drawing on police and other data and applying social network analysis, the Chicago police department assembled a list of roughly 400 individuals identified by certain factors as likely to be involved in violent crime. As a result, police have a heightened awareness of particular individuals that might reflect factors beyond charges and convictions that are part of the public record.[78]

Predictive analytics are also being used in other areas of criminal justice. In Philadelphia, police are using software designed to predict which parolees are more likely to commit a crime after release from prison and thus should have greater supervision.[79] The software uses about two dozen variables, including age, criminal history, and geographic location.

These new techniques have come with considerable controversy about how and when they should be deployed.[80] This technology can help more precisely allocate law enforcement and other public resources, which can lead to the prevention of harmful

---

[76] The National Institute of Justice, the Department of Justice's research, development, and evaluation agency, provides detailed information on the use of predictive policing at law enforcement agencies. For more information, visit www.nij.gov/topics/law-enforcement/strategies/predictive-policing.

[77] Andree G. Ferguson, "Big Data and Predictive Reasonable Suspicion," 163 *University of Pennsylvania Law Review*, April 2014, http://ssrn.com/abstract=2394683.

[78] The application of this particular predictive policing technology emerged out of a series of grants issued by the National Institute of Justice the Chicago Police Department, most recently involving Miles Wernick as technical investigator. For more information, see http://www.nij.gov/topics/law-enforcement/strategies/predictive-policing/Pages/research.aspx.

[79] For more information on government crime prediction using statistical methods, refer to Eric Holder, Mary Lou Leary, and Greg Ridgeway, "Predicting Recidivism Risk: New Tool in Philadelphia Shows Great Promise," *National Criminal Justice Reference Service*, February 2013, https://ncjrs.gov/pdffiles1/nij/240695.pdf.

[80] Controversial aspects of the Chicago pilot's methodology are captured by in Jay Stanley, "Chicago Police 'Heat List' Renews Old Fears About Government Flagging and Tagging," *American Civil Liberties Union*, February 2014, https://www.aclu.org/blog/technology-and-liberty/chicago-police-heat-list-renews-old-fears-about-government-flagging-and; Whet Moser, The Small Social Networks at the Heart of Chicago Violence," *Chicago Magazine,* December 9, 2013, http://www.chicagomag.com/city-life/December-2013/The-Small-Social-Networks-at-the-Heart-of-Chicago-Violence.

crimes. At the same time, our Constitution and Bill of Rights grant certain rights that must not be abridged.

Police departments' potential use of a new array of data and algorithms to try to predict criminal propensities and redirect police powers in advance of criminal activity has important consequences. It requires careful review of how we define "individualized suspicion," which is the constitutional predicate of surveillance and search.[81] The presence and persistence of authority, and the reasonable belief that one's activities, movements, and personal affiliations are being monitored by law enforcement, can have a chilling effect on rights of free speech and association. The next section considers where changes in technology introduce tension within particular areas of the law.

Implications of Big Data Technology for Privacy Law

Access to Data Held by Third Parties

Personal documents and records have evolved from paper kept in the home, to electronic files held on the hard drive of a computer in the home, to many different kinds of computer files kept both locally and in cloud repositories accessed across multiple devices within and outside the home. As remote processing and cloud storage technologies increasingly become the norm for personal computing and records management, we must take measure of the how the law accounts for these developments.

Whether an individual reasonably expects an act to be private has framed much of our thinking about what protections are deserved. As Justice Potter Stewart in the 1967 Katz majority opinion noted: "[T]he Fourth Amendment protects people, not places. What a person knowingly exposes to the public, even in his own home or office, is not a subject of Fourth Amendment protection…But what he seeks to preserve as private, even in an area accessible to the public, may be constitutionally protected."[82]

Two later Supreme Court decisions further elaborated on how the Fourth Amendment applies to information that is shared with third parties. In *United States v. Miller*, in 1976, the Court found that the Fourth Amendment does not prohibit the government from obtaining "information revealed to a third-party and conveyed by him to government authorities, even if the information is revealed on the assumption that it will be used only for a limited purpose and the confidence placed in the third-party will not be betrayed."[83] Three years later, the Supreme Court held in *Smith v. Maryland* that the telephone numbers a person dials are not protected by a reasonable expectation of privacy because the caller voluntarily conveys dialing information to the phone company. The Court again affirmed

---

[81] Though some argue big data analysis is merely a new way to expand the scope of what can be considered "suspicion," the program in question uses an algorithmic calculation heavily reliant on an individual's associations without other criminal pretext.

[82] *Katz v. United States*, 389 U.S. 347, 351-52 (1967).

[83] *United States v. Miller*, 425 U.S. 435, 443 (1976).

that it had "consistently . . . held that a person has no legitimate expectation of privacy in information he voluntarily turns over to third parties."[84]

Miller and *Smith* are often cited as the Supreme Court's foundational "third-party doctrine" cases. For decades, this doctrine has maintained that when an individual voluntarily shares information with third parties, like telephone companies, banks, or even other individuals, the government can acquire that information from the third-party absent a warrant without violating the individual's Fourth Amendment rights. Law enforcement continues to rely on the third-party doctrine to obtain information that can be critical in criminal and national security investigations that keep the American people safe, and federal courts continue to apply the doctrine to both tangible and electronic information in a wide variety of contexts.

Against this backdrop, Congress and state legislatures have enacted statutes that provide additional safeguards for certain types of information, such as the Privacy Act of 1974 protecting personal information held by the federal government; the Electronic Communications Privacy Act of 1986 protecting (among other things) stored electronic communications; and the Pen/Trap Act protecting (among other things) dialing information for phone calls. These legislative measures provide statutory protection in the absence of a strong Fourth Amendment right to protect records held by third parties.

In light of technological advances, especially the creation of exponentially more electronic records about personal interactions, some commentators have called for a reexamination of third-party doctrine.[85] In 2010, the Sixth Circuit Court of Appeals in *United States v. Warshak* held that a subscriber has a reasonable expectation of privacy in his or her email communications, "analogous to a letter or a phone call" and that the government may not compel a commercial internet service provider to turn over the contents of a subscriber's emails without first obtaining a warrant based on probable cause.[86] In a recent Supreme Court case, Justice Sotomayor expressed the view in her concurring opinion that current practices around information disclosure to third parties are "ill-suited to the digital age, in which people reveal a great deal of information about themselves to third parties in the course of carrying out mundane tasks."[87]

Although we are not aware of any courts that have ruled that electronic content of communications can be accessed with less than a warrant, except with the consent of the user, since the *Warshak* case, the third-party doctrine has continued to apply to metada-

---

[84] *Smith v. Maryland*, 442 U.S. 735, 743-44 (1979).

[85] Fred Cate and C. Ben Dutton, "Comments to the 60-Day Cybersecurity Review," *Center for Applied Cybersecurity Research*, March 2009, http://www.whitehouse.gov/files/documents/cyber/Center%20for%20Applied%20Cybersecurity%20Research%20-%20Cybersecurity%20Comments.Cate.pdf; Randy Reitman, "Deep Dive: Updating the Electronic Communications Privacy Act," *Electronic Frontier Foundation*, December 2012, https://www.eff.org/deeplinks/2012/12/deep-dive-updating-electronic-communications-privacy-act.

[86] *United States v. Warshak*, 631 F.3d 266 (6th Cir. 2010).

[87] This assertion was not part of the Supreme Court's holding, but emphasizes the emerging discussion of third-party doctrine. *United States v. Jones*, 132 S.Ct. 945, 957 (2012) (Sotomayor, J., concurring).

ta of such communication and has been adapted and applied to cell-site location information and WiFi signals.[88]

This review of big data and privacy has cast even more light on the profound issues of privacy, market confidence, and rule of law raised by the manner in which the government compels the disclosure of electronic data. We will continually need to examine our laws and policy to keep pace with technology, and should consider how the protection of content data stored remotely, for instance with a cloud provider, should relate to the protection of content data stored in a home office or on a hard drive. This is true of emails, text messages, and other communications platforms, which over the past 30 years have become an important means of private personal correspondence, and are most often stored remotely.

Data and Metadata

The average American transacts with businesses in one form or another multiple times a day, from purchasing goods to uploading digital photos. These interactions create records, some of which, like pharmacy purchases, contain intimate personal information. In the course of ordinary activities, users also emit lots of "digital exhaust," or trace data, that leaves behind more fragmentary bits of information, such as the geographical coordinates of a cell phone transmission or an IP address in a server log. The advent of more powerful analytics, which can discern quite a bit from even small and disconnected pieces of data, raises the possibility that data gathered and held by third parties can be amalgamated and analyzed in ways that reveal even more information about individuals. What protections this material and the information derived from it merit is now a pressing question.

An equally profound question is whether certain types of data—specifically the "metadata" or transactions records about communications and documents, versus the content of those communications and documents—should be accorded stronger privacy protections than they are currently. "Metadata" is a term describing the character of the data itself. The classic example comes from telecommunications. The phone numbers originating and terminating a call, as metadata, are considered less revealing than the conversation itself and have been accorded different privacy protections. Today, with the advent of big data, both the premise and policy may not always be so straightforward.

---

[88] The doctrine has been adapted and applied to cell-site location information multiple times, most recently by the Fifth Circuit in *In re Application of the United States for Historical Cell Site Data,* 724 F.3d 600 (5th Cir. 2013) (finding cell site data may be obtained without a probable cause warrant); *United States v. Norris,* No. 2:11-CR-00188-KJM, 2013 WL 4737197 (E.D. Cal. Sept. 3, 2013) (finding defendant who hacked a private wireless network had no reasonable expectation of privacy in his transmissions over that network). Moreover, leading commentators have argued for the continuing vitality of the third-party doctrine in the modern era, including Professor Orin Kerr in Orin S. Kerr, "The Case for the Third-Party Doctrine," 107 *Michigan Law Review* 561 (2009), and Orin S. Kerr, "Defending the Third-Party Doctrine: A Response to Epstein and Murphy," 24 *Berkeley Technology Law Journal* 1229 (2009). *See also United States v. Perrine,* 518 F.3d 1196, 1204 (10th Cir. 2008); *United States v. Forrester,* 512 F.3d 500, 510 (9th Cir. 2008).

Experts seem divided on this issue, but those who argue that metadata today raises more sensitivities than in the past make a sufficiently compelling case to motivate review of policy on the matter. In the intelligence context, the President has already directed his Intelligence Advisory Board to consider the issue, and offer recommendations about the long-term viability of current assumptions about metadata and privacy. This review recommends that the government should broaden that examination beyond intelligence and consider the extent to which data and information should receive legal or other protections on the basis of how much it reveals about individuals.

Government Use of Commercial Data Services

Powerful private-sector profiling and data-mining technologies are not only used for commercial purposes. State, local, and federal agencies purchase access to many kinds of private databases for legitimate public uses, from land management to administering benefits. The sources of data that flow into these products are sometimes not publicly disclosed or may even be shielded as proprietary business information. Some legal scholars and privacy advocates have already raised concerns about the use of commercial data service products by the government, including law enforcement and intelligence agencies.[89]

The Department of the Treasury has been working to implement a program to help prevent waste, fraud, and abuse in federal spending by reducing the number of payments made to the wrong person, for the wrong amount, or without the proper paperwork. To provide federal agencies with a "one-stop-shop" to check various databases and identify ineligible recipients or prevent fraud or errors, the Treasury launched a "Do Not Pay" portal. While all of the current databases available on the portal are government databases, Treasury anticipates that commercial databases may eventually be useful as well.

To assist the Treasury, the Office of Management and Budget issued substantial guidance to ensure that individual privacy is fully protected in the program.[90] The guidance recognized that commercial data sources "may also present new or increased privacy risks, such as databases with inaccurate or out-of-date information." The guidelines require any commercial databases included in the Do Not Pay portal to be reviewed and approved following a 30-day period of public notice and comment. Among other requirements, the database must be relevant and necessary to the program, must be sufficiently accurate to ensure fairness to the individuals included in the database, and must

---

[89] See Robert Gellman and Pam Dixon, "Data Brokers and the Federal Government: A New Front in the Battle for Privacy Opens," *World Privacy Forum Report*, Oct. 30, 2013; Chris Hoofnagle, "Big Brother's Little Helpers: How Choicepoint and Other Commercial Data Brokers Collect, Process, and Package Your Data for Law Enforcement," 29 *North Carolina Journal of International Law and Commercial Regulation* 595 (2003); Jon Michaels, "All the President's Spies: Private-Public Intelligence Partnerships in the War on Terror," 96 *California Law Review* 901 (2008).

[90] Office of Management and Budget memorandum M-13-20, *Protecting Privacy while Reducing Improper Payments with the Do Not Pay Initiative* (Aug. 13, 2013), http://www.whitehouse.gov/sites/default/files/omb/memoranda/2013/m-13-20.pdf.

not contain information that describes how any individual exercises rights guaranteed by the First Amendment, unless use of the data is expressly authorized by statute.

Given the increasing range of sensitive information available about individuals through commercial sources, this guidance is a significant step to ensure privacy protections when private-sector data is used to inform government decision-making. Similar OMB guidance should be considered for a wider range of agencies and programs, so the protections Americans have come to expect from their government exist regardless of where data originates.

Insider Threat and Continuous Evaluation

The 2013 shooting at the Washington Navy Yard facility by a contract employee who held a secret security clearance despite a record of arrests and troubling behavior has added urgency to ongoing efforts to more frequently evaluate employees who hold special positions of public trust.[91] It was the latest in a string of troubling breaches and acts of violence by insiders who held security clearances, including Chelsea Manning's disclosures to WikiLeaks, the Fort Hood shooting by Major Nidal Hasan, and the most serious breach in the history of U.S. intelligence, the release of classified National Security Agency documents by Edward Snowden.

Federal government employees and contractors go through different levels of investigation, depending on the level of risk, sensitivity of their position, or their need to access sensitive facilities or systems. Currently, employees and contractors who hold "top secret" clearances are reinvestigated every five years, and those holding "secret" clearances every ten. These lengthy gaps do not allow agencies to discover new and noteworthy information about an employee in a timely manner.

Pilot programs have demonstrated the efficacy of using automated queries of appropriate official and commercial databases and social media to identify violations or irregularities, known as "derogatory information," that may call into question a person's suitability to continue serving in a sensitive position. The Department of Defense, for instance, recently conducted a pilot of what it calls the "Automated Continuous Evaluation System." The pilot examined a sample of 3,370 Army service members, civilian employees, and contractor personnel, and identified that 21.7 percent of the tested population had previously unreported derogatory information that had developed since the last investigation. For 99 individuals, the pilot surfaced serious financial, domestic abuse, drug abuse, or allegations of prostitution that resulted in the revocation or suspension of their clearances.[92]

---

[91] Department of Defense, *Security From Within: A Report of the Independent Review of the Washington Navy Yard Shooting*, November 2013, http://www.defense.gov/pubs/Independent-Review-of-the-WNY-Shooting-14-Nov-2013.pdf; Department of Defense, Under Secretary of Defense for Intelligence, *Internal Review of the Washington Navy Yard Shooting: A Report to the Secretary of Defense*, November, 2013, http://www.defense.gov/pubs/DoD-Internal-Review-of-the-WNY-Shooting-20-Nov-2013.pdf.
[92] Ibid.

The Administration recently released a review of suitability and security practices which called for expanding continuous evaluation capabilities across the federal government.[93] The Administration's report recommends adopting practices across all agencies and security levels, although the exact extent of the information that will be used in these programs, especially social media sources, is still being determined.

These reforms will create a fundamentally different process for granting and maintaining security clearances that stands to enhance our security and safety. As the Administration works to expand the use of continuous evaluation across federal agencies, the privacy of employees and contractors will have to be carefully considered. The ability to refute or correct errant information that triggers reviews must be built into the process for appealing denials or revocations of clearance. We must ensure the big data analytics powering continuous evaluation are used in ways that protect the public as well as the civil liberties and privacy rights of those who serve on their behalf.

Conclusion

When wrestling with the vexing issues big data raises in the public sector, it can be easy to lose sight of the tremendous opportunities these technologies offer to improve public services, grow the economy, and improve the health and safety of our communities. These opportunities are real and must be kept at the center of the conversation about big data.

Big data holds enormous power to make the provision of services more efficient across the entire spectrum of government activity and to detect fraud, waste, and abuse at higher rates. Big data can also help create entirely new forms of value. New sources of precise data about weather patterns can provide meaningful scientific insights about climate change, while the ability to understand energy and natural resource use can lead to greater efficiency and reduce overall consumption. The movement, storage, and analysis of data all stands to grow more efficient and powerful. The Department of Energy, for instance, is working to develop computer memory and supercomputing frameworks that will in turn yield entire new classes of analytics tools, driving the big data revolution faster still.

There is virtually no part of government that does not stand serve citizens better. The big data revolution will take hold across the entire government, not merely in departments and agencies that already have missions involving science and technology. Those departments and agencies that have not historically made wide use of advanced data analytics have perhaps the most significant opportunity to harness big data to benefit the citizens they serve.

---

[93] Performance Accountability Council, *Suitability and Security Processes Review, Report to the President*, February 2014, http://www.whitehouse.gov/sites/default/files/omb/reports/suitability-and-security-process-review-report.pdf.

The power of big data does not stop at the federal level. It will be equally transformational for states and municipalities. Cities and towns have emerged as some of the most innovative users of big data to improve service delivery. The federal agencies and programs that provide grants and technical assistance to cities, towns, and counties should promote the use of these transformational municipal technologies to the greatest extent possible, replicating the successes pioneered by New York City's Office of Data Analytics and Chicago's Smart Data project.

Making big data work for the public good also takes people with skills that are in short supply and high demand. A recent assessment of the ability of the public and nonprofit sectors to attract and retain technical talent sounded a strong note of alarm.[94] Though there are many young technologists who care deeply about public service and would welcome the chance to work in government, private sector opportunities are so comparatively attractive that these technologists tend to use their skills applying big data in the marketplace rather than the public sector. This means that alongside investments in technology, the federal government must create a more attractive working culture for technologists and remove hiring barriers that keep out the very experts whose creativity and technical imagination is paramount to realizing the full potential of big data in government.

---

[94] Ford and MacArthur Foundation, *A Future or Failure?: The Flow of Technology Talent into Government and Civil Society*, December 2013, http://www.fordfoundation.org/pdfs/news/afutureoffailure.pdf.

IV. Private Sector Management of Data

Big data means big things all across the global economy. In the next two years, the big data technologies and services market is projected to continue its rapid ascent.[95] This chapter considers how big data is shaping the products and services available to consumers and businesses, and highlights some of the challenges that arise when consumers have little insight into how information about them is being collected, analyzed, and used.

The Obama Administration has supported America's leadership position in using big data to spark innovation, productivity, and value in the private sector. However, the near-continuous collection, transfer, and re-purposing of information in a big data world also raises important questions about individual control over personal data and the risks of its use to exploit vulnerable populations. While big data will be a powerful engine for economic growth and innovation, there remains the potential for a disquieting asymmetry between consumers and the companies that control information about them.

Big Data Benefits for Enterprise and Consumer

Big data is creating value for both companies and consumers. The benefits of big data can be felt across a range of sectors, in both large and small firms, as access to data and the tools for processing it are further democratized. In large enterprises, there are several drivers of investment in big data technologies: the ability to analyze operational and transactional data, to glean insights into the behavior of online customers, to bring new and exceedingly complex products to market, and to derive deeper understanding from machines and devices within organizations.

Technology companies are using big data to analyze millions of voice samples to deliver more reliable and accurate voice interfaces. Banks are using big data techniques to improve fraud detection. Health care providers are leveraging more detailed data to improve patient treatment. Big data is being used by manufacturers to improve warranty management and equipment monitoring, as well as to optimize the logistics of getting their products to market. Retailers are harnessing a wide range of customer interactions, both online and offline, in order to provide more tailored recommendations and optimal pricing.[96]

For consumers, big data is fueling an expansion of products and services that impact their daily lives. It is enabling cybersecurity experts to protect systems—from credit card

---

[95] Dan Vesset and Henry Morris, *Unlocking the Business Value of Big Data: Infosys BigDataEdge*, IDC, 2013, http://www.infosys.com/bigdataedge/resources/Documents/unlocking-business-value.pdf
[96] Ibid.

readers to electricity grids—by harnessing vast amounts of network and application data and using it to identify anomalies and threats.[97] It is also enabling some of the nearly 29 percent of Americans who are "unbanked" or "underbanked" to qualify for a line of credit by using a wider range of non-traditional information—such as rent payments, utilities, mobile-phone subscriptions, insurance, child care, and tuition—to establish creditworthiness.[98]

These new technologies are sensor-rich and embedded in networks. Lighting infrastructure can now detect sound, speed, temperature, and even carbon monoxide levels, and will draw data from car parks, schools, and along public streets to improve energy efficiency and public safety. Vehicles record and report a spectrum of driving and usage data that will pave the way for advanced transportation systems and improved safety. Home appliances can now tell us when to dim our lights from a thousand miles away. These are the kinds of changes that policies must accommodate. The Federal Trade Commission has already begun working to frame the policy questions raised by the Internet of Things, building on their long history of protecting consumers as new technologies come online.

The next sections discuss the online advertising and data services industries, each of which have significant histories using large datasets within long-established regulatory frameworks.

The Advertising-Supported Ecosystem

Since the earliest days of the commercial web, online advertising has been a vital driver of the growth of the Internet. One study estimated that the ad-supported Internet sustains millions of jobs in the United States and that the interactive marketing industry contributes billions to the U.S. economy each year.[99] This is a natural industry for big data to take root in and flourish. Increasingly precise data about consumers—where they are, what devices they use, and literally hundreds of categories of their interests—coupled with powerful analysis have enabled advertisers to more efficiently reach customers. Expensive television slots or full-page national magazine ads seem crude compared to the precisely segmented and instantaneously measured online ad marketplace. One study suggests that advertisers are willing to pay a premium of between 60 and 200 percent for online targeted advertising.[100]

---

[97] Centre for Information Policy Leadership, *Big Data and Analytics: Seeking Foundations for Effective Privacy Guidance*, February 2013, p. 3-4, http://www.hunton.com/files/Uploads/Documents/News_files/Big_Data_and_Analytics_February_2013.pdf.
[98] FDIC, *2011 FDIC National Survey of Unbanked and Underbanked Households*, 2012, http://www.fdic.gov/householdsurvey/2012_unbankedreport_execsumm.pdf.
[99] John Deighton and Leora Kornfeld, *Economic Value of the Advertising-Supported Internet Ecosystem*, Interactive Advertising Bureau, 2012, http://www.iab.net/economicvalue.
[100] J. Howard Beales and Jeffrey Eisenach, *An Empirical Analysis Of The Value Of Information Sharing in the Market for Online Content*, Navigant Economics, 2014, https://www.aboutads.info/resource/fullvalueinfostudy.pdf.

Consumers are reaping the benefits of a robust digital ecosystem that offers a broad array of free content, products, and services. The Internet also puts national or international advertising within reach of not just major companies, but mom-and-pop stores and fledgling brands. As a result, consumers are getting better, more useful ads from—and access to—a wider range of businesses, in a marketplace that is ultimately more competitive and innovative.

Many different actors play a role in making this ecosystem work, including the consumer, the companies they engage with directly, and an array of other entities that provide services like analytics or security, or derive and share data. Standing between the publisher of the website a user visits and the advertiser paying for the ad displayed on the user's page are a dizzying array of other companies. Advertising networks and ad exchanges facilitate transactions between the publishers and the advertisers. Ad content and campaigns are created and placed by agencies, optimizers, and media planners. Ad performance is measured and analyzed by yet another set of specialized companies.[101]

In general, the companies with which a consumer engages directly—news websites, social media, or online or offline retailers—are called "first parties," as they collect information directly from the consumer. But as described above, a broad range of companies may gather information indirectly because they are in the business of processing data on behalf of the first-party company or may have access to data—most often in an aggregated or de-identified form—as part of a different business relationship. These "third-party" companies include the many "middle players" in the digital ecosystem, as well as financial transaction companies that handle payment processing, companies that fill orders, and others. The first parties may use the data themselves, or resell it to others to develop advertising profiles or for other uses. Users, more often than not, do not understand the degree to which they are a commodity in each level of this marketplace.

The Consumer and the Challenge of Transparency

For well over a decade, the online advertising industry has worked to provide consumers choice and transparency in a self-regulatory framework. Starting at the edges of the ecosystem, where the consumer can identify the website publisher and the advertiser whose ads are served, privacy policies and other forms of notice have served to inform consumers how their information is used. Under this self-regulatory regime, companies agree to a set of principles when engaged in "behavioral" or multi-site advertising where they collect information about user activities over time and across different websites in order to infer user preferences. These principles include requiring notice to the user about their data collection practices; providing options for users to opt out of some forms of tracking; limiting the use of sensitive information, such as children's information or medical or financial data; and a requirement to delete or de-identify data.

---

[101] LUMA Partners, "Display Lumascape," http://www.lumapartners.com/lumascapes/display-ad-tech-lumascape.

Technologies to improve transparency and privacy choices online have been slow to develop, and for many reasons have not been used widely by consumers. For example, under the self-regulatory regime adopted by advertisers and ad networks, many online behavioral ads include a standardized icon that indicates information is being collected for purposes of behavioral ad targeting, and links to a page where the consumer can opt-out of such collection.[102] According to the online advertising industry, this icon has appeared on ads billions of times, but only a tiny fraction of users utilize this feature or understand its meaning. Advertising networks operated by some of the largest online companies have also offered users detailed dashboards for seeing the basis on which they are targeted for advertising and giving them the ability to opt out.[103] These, too, have received little consumer attention. There are many theories about why users do not make use of these privacy features. Some assert that the privacy tools are hidden or too difficult for most users to navigate.[104] Others argue that users have "privacy fatigue" from the barrage of privacy policies and settings they must wade through to simply use a service.[105] It is also possible that most of the public is not very bothered by personalized ads when they enjoy a robust selection of free content, products, and services.

As we look ahead at the rising trajectory of information collection across many sources and the ability to target advertising with greater precision, the challenge to consumer transparency and meaningful choice deepens. Even employing relatively straightforward technical measures that would provide consumers with greater control over how data flows between their web browser and the servers of the webpages they visit for advertising purposes—what has become known as the "Do Not Track" browser setting—can be problematic because anti-fraud and online security activities now rely on these same data flows to track and prevent malicious activity.

The Challenge with Do Not Track

The idea behind a Do Not Track privacy setting is to provide an easy-to-use solution that empowers consumers to limit the tracking of their activities across websites. Some browsers provide a kind of Do Not Track capability by blocking third-party cookies by default, or allowing consumers to choose to do so. Some browsers also allow consumers to send a signal instructing services not to track them. While Do Not Track technology is fairly straightforward, attempts to build consensus around the policy requirements for the

---

[102] For information about the industry's opt-out program, see http://www.youradchoices.com/..

[103] See Google Ads Settings at http://www.google.com/settings/ads; Yahoo! Ads Interest Manager at https://info.yahoo.com/privacy/us/yahoo/opt_out/targeting/; Microsoft at http://choice.microsoft.com/en-us/opt-out.

[104] See, e.g., Pedro Leon, Blase Ur, Richard Shay, Yang Wang, Rebecca Balebako, and Lorrie Cranor, "Why Johnny Can't Opt Out: a Usability Evaluation of Tools to Limit Online Behavioral Advertising," Proceedings of the SIGCHI Conference on Human Factors in Computing Systems, 2012, http://dl.acm.org/citation.cfm?doid=2207676.2207759.

[105] See, e.g., Sarah Kidner, "Privacy Fatigue Hits Facebook: Have You Updated Your Settings?," *Which? Conversation*, Oct. 18, 2011, http://conversation.which.co.uk/technology/facebook-privacy-settings-privacy-fatigue/; Aleecia McDonald and Lorrie Cranor, "The Cost of Reading Privacy Policies," 4 *Information Society: A Journal of Law and Policy for the Information Society*, 543, 544, 564 (2008).

websites receiving visits by users with Do Not Track technology enabled have proven far more difficult. Some websites voluntarily agreed to honor the wishes of visitors with Do Not Track indicators, but others have not, or have adopted policies that still permit partial tracking—muddling expectations for consumers and frustrating privacy advocates.

A working group of the World Wide Web Consortium, which included technologists, developers, advertising industry representatives, and privacy advocates, worked to craft a standard for implementation of the Do Not Track signal for more than three years. Recently, the working group released a final candidate for a technical Do Not Track specification, which will now go to the larger community to consider for approval.

In the meantime, the European Union amended its E-Privacy Directive in 2009 to require user consent to the use of cookies and other online tracking devices, unless they are "strictly necessary for delivery of a service requested by the user," such as an online shopping cart. Compliance with the Directive has been uneven, although many European company websites now obtain a one-time explicit consent for the use of cookies—a solution that is widely acknowledged as clunky and which has been criticized in some circles as not providing the user the meaningful choice about privacy first envisioned by the directive.

While imperfect, these efforts reflect a growing interest in creating a technological means to allow individuals to control how commercial entities collect and use information about them.

The Data Services Sector

Alongside firms that focus primarily on online advertising are a related set of businesses that offer broader services drawn from information about consumers, public records, and other data sets. The "data services" sector—sometimes called "data brokers"— encompasses a class of businesses that collect data across many sources, aggregate and analyze it, and then share that information, or information derived from it. Typically, these companies have no direct relationship with the consumers whose information they collect. Instead, they offer services to other businesses or government agencies, including marketing products, verifying an individual's identity, providing "people search" services, or detecting fraud. Some of these companies also have a specific line of business as "consumer reporting agencies," which provide reports for purposes of credit applications, insurance, employment, or health care reports.

From a regulatory standpoint, data services fall into three broad categories:

1. Consumer reporting functions regulated under the Fair Credit Reporting Act, which generally keep the data, analysis, and reporting collected and used for these purposes in a separate system and under specific compliance rules apart from the rest of their data services operations.

2. Risk mitigation services such as identity verification, fraud detection and people-search or look up services; and

3. Marketing services to identify potential customers, enhance ad targeting information, and other advertising-related services.

The Fair Credit Reporting Act, as discussed in Chapter 2, provides affirmative rights to consumers. Consumer reporting agencies that provide reports for determining eligibility for credit, insurance, or employment, are required under the Fair Credit Reporting Act or the Equal Credit Opportunity Act to inform consumers when an adverse action, such as a denial or higher cost of credit, is taken against them based on a report. By law, consumers also have a right to know what is in their file, what their credit score is, and how to correct or delete inaccurate information.[106] The Fair Credit Reporting Act mandates that credit reporting agencies remove negative information after certain periods, such that late payments and tax liens are deleted from a consumer's file after seven years and bankruptcies after ten. Certain types of information—such as race, gender and religion—may not be used as factors to determine creditworthiness.

These statutory rights do not exist for risk mitigation or marketing services. As a matter of practice, data services companies may provide access and correction mechanisms to consumers for the information used in identity verification. In the context of marketing services, some companies permit consumers to opt-out of having their personal information used in marketing services.

Unregulated Data Broker Services

To assist marketers, data brokers can provide a profile of a consumer who may interact with a brand or seek services across many different channels, from online web presence to social media to mobile engagement. Data brokers aggregate purchase patterns, activities on a website, mobile, social media, ad network interactions, or direct customer support, and then further "enhance" it with information from public records or other commercially available sources. That information is used to develop a profile of a customer, whose activities or engagements can then be monitored to help the marketer pinpoint the message to send and the right moment to send it.

These profiles can be exceptionally detailed, containing upwards of thousands of pieces of data. Some large data firms have profiles on hundreds of millions of consumers. They algorithmically analyze this information to segment customers into precise categories, often with illustrative names that help their business customers identify populations for targeted advertising. Some of these categories include "Ethnic Second-City Strugglers," "Retiring on Empty: Singles," "Tough Start: Young Single Parents," "Credit Crunched: City Families," and "Rural and Barely Making It."[107] These products include factual information about individuals as well as "modeled" elements inferred from other data. Data brokers then sell "original lists" of consumers who fit particular criteria. They may also offer a "data append" service whereby companies can buy additional data about particu-

[106] Federal Trade Commission, "A Summary of Your Rights Under the Fair Credit Reporting Act," http://www.consumer.ftc.gov/articles/pdf-0096-fair-credit-reporting-act.pdf.
[107] U.S. Senate Committee on Commerce, Science & Transportation, Majority Staff, "A Review of the Data Broker Industry: Collection, Use, and Sale of Consumer Data for Marketing Purposes," p. ii, December 18, 2013.

lar customers to help them build out more complete profiles of individuals on whom they maintain information.[108]

What is a Credit Reporting Agency?

Since the 1950s, credit reporting companies–now known as "consumer reporting agencies"–have collected information and provided reports on individuals that are used to decide eligibility for credit, insurance or a job. In one typical scenario, a credit reporting agency collects information about an individual's credit history, such as whether they pay their bills on time, how many and what kind of accounts they hold and for how long, whether they've been the subject of collection actions, and whether they have outstanding debt. The agency then uses a statistical program to compare this information to the loan repayment history of consumers with similar profiles and assigns a score that reflects the individual's creditworthiness: how likely it is that he or she will repay a loan and make timely payments. This score facilitates consumers' ability to buy a home or car or otherwise engage in the economy by becoming a basis for creditors' decisions about whether to provide credit to the consumer, and on what terms.

While this precise profiling of consumer attributes yields benefits, it also represents a powerful capacity on the part of the private sector to collect information and use that information to algorithmically profile an individual, possibly without the individual's knowledge or consent. This application of big data technology, if used improperly, irresponsibly, or nefariously, could have significant ramifications for targeted individuals. In its 2012 Privacy Report, the Federal Trade Commission recommended that data brokers become more transparent in the services that are not already covered by the Fair Credit Report Act, and provide consumers with reasonable access to and choices about data maintained about them, in proportion to the sensitivity of data and how it is used.[109]

Algorithms, Alternative Scoring and the Specter of Discrimination

The business models and big data strategies now being built around the collection and use of consumer data, particularly among the "third-party" data services companies, raise important questions about how to ensure transparency and accountability in these practices. Powerful algorithms can unlock value in the vast troves of information available to businesses, and can help empower consumers, but also raise the potential of encoding discrimination in automated decisions. Fueled by greater access to data and powerful analytics, there are now a host of products that "score" individuals beyond the scope of traditional credit scores, which are regulated by law.[110] These products attempt to statistically characterize everything from a consumer's ability to pay to whether, on the basis of their social media posts, they are a "social influencer" or "socially influenced."

---

[108] Ibid at 22.

[109] Federal Trade Commission, *Protecting Consumer Privacy in an Era of Rapid Change: Recommendations for Business and Consumers*, 2012, http://www.ftc.gov/reports/protecting-consumer-privacy-era-rapid-change-recommendations-businesses-policymakers.

[110] Frank Pasquale, *The Black Box Society: The Secret Algorithm Behind Money and Information*, (Harvard University Press, 2014).

While these scores may be generated for marketing purposes, they can also in practice be used similarly to regulated credit scores in ways that influence an individuals' opportunities to find housing, forecast their job security, or estimate their health, outside of the protections of the Fair Credit Reporting Act or Equal Credit Opportunity Act.[111] Details on what types of data are included in these scores and the algorithms used for assigning attributes to an individual are held closely by companies and largely invisible to consumers. That means there is often no meaningful avenue for either identifying harms or holding any entity in the decision-making chain accountable.

Because of this lack of transparency and accountability, individuals have little recourse to understand or contest the information that has been gathered about them or what that data, after analysis, suggests.[112] Nor is there an industry-wide portal for consumers to communicate with data services companies, as the online advertising industry voluntarily provides and the Fair Credit Reporting Act requires for regulated entities. This can be particularly harmful to victims of identity theft who have ongoing errors or omissions impacting their scores and, as a result, their ability to engage in commerce.

What is an algorithm?

In simple terms, an algorithm is defined by a sequence of steps and instructions that can be applied to data. Algorithms generate categories for filtering information, operate on data, look for patterns and relationships, or generally assist in the analysis of information. The steps taken by an algorithm are informed by the author's knowledge, motives, biases, and desired outcomes. The output of an algorithm may not reveal any of those elements, nor may it reveal the probability of a mistaken outcome, arbitrary choice, or the degree of uncertainty in the judgment it produces. So-called "learning algorithms" which underpin everything from recommendation engines to content filters evolve with the datasets that run through them, assigning different weights to each variable. The final computer-generated product or decision—used for everything from predicting behavior to denying opportunity—can mask prejudices while maintaining a patina of scientific objectivity.

For all of these reasons, the civil rights community is concerned that such algorithmic decisions raise the specter of "redlining" in the digital economy—the potential to discriminate against the most vulnerable classes of our society under the guise of neutral algorithms.[113] Recently, some offline retailers were found to be using an algorithm that generated different discounts for the same product to people based on where they believed

---

[111] Pam Dixon and Robert Gellman, "The Scoring of America: How Secret Consumer Scores Threaten Your Privacy and Your Future," *World Privacy Forum*, April 2014, http://www.worldprivacyforum.org/wp-content/uploads/2014/04/WPF_Scoring_of_America_April2014_fs.pdf.

[112] The Government Accounting Office conducted a gap analysis of privacy laws and regulation in its September 2013 report on Information Resellers. See GAO, *Information Resellers: Consumer Privacy Framework Needs to Reflect Changes in Technology and the Marketplace*, GAO-13-663, 2013, http://www.gao.gov/assets/660/658151.pdf.

[113] The Leadership Conference on Civil and Human Rights, "Civil Rights Principles for the Era of Big Data," http://www.civilrights.org/press/2014/civil-rights-principles-big-data.html.

the customer was located. While it may be that the price differences were driven by the lack of competition in certain neighborhoods, in practice, people in higher-income areas received higher discounts than people in lower-income areas.[114]

There are perfectly legitimate reasons to offer different prices for the same products in different places. But the ability to segment the population and to stratify consumer experiences so seamlessly as to be almost undetectable demands greater review, especially when it comes to the practice of differential pricing and other potentially discriminatory practices. It will also be important to examine how algorithmically-driven decisions might exacerbate existing socio-economic disparities beyond the pricing of goods and services, including in education and workforce settings.

Conclusion

The advertising-supported Internet creates enormous value for consumers by providing access to useful services, news, and entertainment at no financial cost. The ability to more precisely target advertisements is of enormous value to companies, which can efficiently reach audiences that are more likely to purchase their goods and services. However, private-sector uses of big data must ensure vulnerable classes are not unfairly targeted. The increasing use of algorithms to make eligibility decisions must be carefully monitored for potential discriminatory outcomes for disadvantaged groups, even absent discriminatory intent. The Federal Trade Commission should be commended for their continued engagement with industry and the public on this complex topic and should continue its plans to focus further attention on emerging practices in the data broker industry. We look forward to their forthcoming report on this important topic. Additional work should be done to identify practical ways of increasing consumer access to information about unregulated consumer scoring, with particular emphasis on the ability to correct or suppress inaccurate information. Likewise, additional research in measuring adverse outcomes due to the use of scores or algorithms is needed to understand the impacts these tools are having and will have in both the private and public sector as their use grows.

---

[114] Jennifer Valentino-Devries and Jeremy Singer-Vine, "Websites Vary Prices, Deals Based on Users' Information," *The Wall Street Journal*, December 24, 2012, http://online.wsj.com/news/articles/SB10001424127887323777204578189391813881534.

V. Toward a Policy Framework for Big Data

In what feels like the blink of an eye, the information age has fundamentally reconfigured how data affects individual lives and the broader economy. More than 6,000 data centers dot the globe. International data flows are continuous and multidirectional. To a greater degree than ever before, this data is being harnessed by businesses, governments, and entrepreneurs to improve the services they deliver and enhance how people live and work.

Big data applications create social and economic value on a scale that, collectively, is of strategic importance for the nation. Technological innovation is the animating force of the American economy. In the years to come, big data will foster significant productivity gains in industry and manufacturing, further accelerating the integration of the industrial and information economies.

Government should support the development of big data technologies with the full suite of policy instruments in its toolkit. Agencies must continue advancing the Administration's Open Data initiative. The federal government should also invest in research and development to support big data technologies, especially as they apply to education, health care, and energy. As the preceding chapters have documented, adjusting existing policies will make possible certain new applications of big data that are clearly in the public interest, particularly in health care. The policy framework for big data will require cooperation between the public and private sectors to accelerate the revolution that is underway and identify barriers that ought to be removed for innovations driven by big data to flourish.

Like other transformative factors of production, big data generates value differently for individuals, organizations, and society. While many applications of big data are unequivocally beneficial, some of its uses impact privacy and other core values of fairness, equity, and autonomy.

Big data technologies enable data collection that is more ubiquitous, invasive, and valuable. This new cache of collected and derived data is of huge potential benefit but is also unevenly regulated. Certain private and public institutions have access to more data and more resources to compute it, potentially heightening asymmetries between institutions and individuals.

It is the responsibility of government to ensure that transformative technologies are used fairly and employed in all areas where they can achieve public good. Four areas in particular emerge as places for further policy exploration:

1. How government can harness big data for the public good while guarding against unacceptable uses against citizens;

2. The extent to which big data alters the consumer landscape in ways that implicate core values;

3. How to protect citizens from new forms of discrimination that may be enabled by big data technologies; and

4. How big data affects the core tenet of modern privacy protection, the notice and consent framework that has been in wide use since the 1970s.

Big Data and the Citizen

Big data will enhance how the government administers public services and enable it to create whole new kinds of value. But big data tools also unquestionably increase the potential of government power to accrue unchecked. Local police departments now have access to surveillance tools more powerful than those used by superpowers during the Cold War. The new means of surveillance that in Justice Alito's evocative analogy deploy "tiny constables" to all areas of life, together with the ways citizens can be profiled by algorithms that redirect police powers, raise many questions about big data's implications for First Amendment rights of free speech and free association.

Many of the laws governing law enforcement access to electronic information were passed by Congress at a time when private papers were largely stored in the home. The Stored Communications Act, which is part of the Electronic Communications Privacy Act (ECPA), articulates the rules for obtaining the content of electronic communications, including email and cloud services. ECPA was originally passed in 1986. It has served to protect the privacy of individuals' stored communications. But with time, some of the lines drawn by the statute have become outdated and no longer reflect ways in which we use technology today. In considering how to update the Act, there are a variety of interests at stake, including privacy interests and the need for law enforcement and civil enforcement agencies to protect public safety and enforce criminal and civil law. Email, text messaging, and other private digital communications have become the principal means of personal correspondence and the cloud is increasingly used to store individuals' files. They should receive commensurate protections.

Similarly, many protections afforded to metadata were calibrated for a time that predated the rise of personal computers, the Internet, mobile phones, and cloud computing. No one imagined then that the traces of digital data left today as a matter of routine can be reassembled to reveal intimate personal details. Today, most law enforcement uses of metadata are still rooted in the "small data" world, such as identifying phone numbers called by a criminal suspect. In the future, metadata that is part of the "big data" world will be increasingly relevant to investigations, raising the question of what protections it should be granted. While today, the content of communications, whether written or verbal, generally receives a high level of legal protection, the level of protection afforded to metadata is less so.

Although the use of big data technologies by the government raises profound issues of how government power should be regulated, big data technologies also hold within them solutions that can enhance accountability, privacy, and the rights of citizens. These include sophisticated methods of tagging data by the authorities under which it was collected or generated; purpose- and user-based access restrictions on this data; tracking which users access what data for what purpose; and algorithms that alert supervisors to possible abuses. All of these methods are being employed in parts of the federal government today to protect the rights of citizens and regulate how big data technologies are used, and more agencies should put them to use. Responsibly employed, big data could lead to an aggregate increase in actual protections for the civil liberties and civil rights afforded of citizens, as well as drive transformation improvements in the provision of public services.

Big Data and the Consumer

The technologies of collection and analysis that fuel big data are being used in every sector of society and the economy. Many of them are trained squarely on people as consumers. One of the most intensely discussed of big data analytics to date has been in the online advertising industry, where it is used to serve customized ads as people browse the web or travel around town with their mobile phone. But the information collected and the uses to which it is put are far broader and quickly changing, with data derived from the real world increasingly being combined with data drawn from online activity.

The end result is a massive increase in the amount of intimate information compiled about individuals. This information is highly valuable to businesses of all kinds. It is bought, bartered, traded, and sold. An entire industry now exists to commoditize the conclusions drawn from that data. Products sold on the market today include dozens of consumer scores on particular individuals that describe attributes, propensities, degrees of social influence over others, financial habits, household wealth, and even suitability as a tenant, job security, and frailty. While some of these scoring efforts are highly regulated, other uses of data are not.

There are enormous benefits associated with the rise of profiling and targeted advertising and the ways consumers can be tracked and offered services as they move through the online and physical world. Advertising and marketing effectively subsidize many free goods on the Internet, fueling an entire industry in software and consumer apps. As one person pointedly remarked during this review, "We don't like putting a quarter into the machine to go do a web search."

Data collection is also vital to securely verify identity online. The data services and financial industries have gone to extraordinary lengths to enable individuals to conduct secure transactions from computers and mobile devices. The same verification technologies that make transaction in the private sector possible also enable citizens to securely interact with the government online, opening a new universe of public services, all accessible from an arm chair.

But there are also costs to organizing the provision of commercial services in this way. Amalgamating so much information about consumers makes data breaches more consequential, highlighting the need for federal data breach legislation to replace a confusing patchwork of state standards. The sheer number of participants in this new, interconnected ecosystem of data collection, storage, aggregation, transfer, and sale can disadvantage consumers. The average consumer is unlikely to be aware of the range of data being collected or held or even to know who holds it; will have few opportunities to engage over the scope or accuracy of data being held about them; and may have limited insight into how this information feeds into algorithms that make decisions about their consumer experience or market access.

When considering what policies will allow big data to flourish in the consumer context, a crucial distinction must be drawn around the ways this collected information gets used. It is one thing for big data to segment consumers for marketing purposes, thereby providing more tailored opportunities to purchase goods and services. It is another, arguably far more serious, matter if this information comes to figure in decisions about a consumer's eligibility for—or the conditions for the provision of—employment, housing, health care, credit, or education.

Big Data and Discrimination

In addition to creating tremendous social good, big data in the hands of government and the private sector can cause many kinds of harms. These harms range from tangible and material harms, such as financial loss, to less tangible harms, such as intrusion into private life and reputational damage. An important conclusion of this study is that big data technologies can cause societal harms beyond damages to privacy, such as discrimination against individuals and groups. This discrimination can be the inadvertent outcome of the way big data technologies are structured and used. It can also be the result of intent to prey on vulnerable classes.

An illustrative example of how one organization ensured that a big data technology did not inadvertently discriminate comes from Boston, where the city developed an experimental app in partnership with the Mayor's Office of New Urban Mechanics.[115] Street Bump is a mobile application that uses a smartphone's accelerometer and GPS feed to collect data about road condition, including potholes, and report them to the city's Public Works Department. It is a marvelous example of how cities are creatively using crowdsourcing to improve service delivery. But the Street Bump team also identified a potential problem with deploying the app to the public. Because the poor and the elderly are less likely to carry smartphones or download the Street Bump app, its release could

---

[115] See New Urban Mechanics, http://www.newurbanmechanics.org/. All information about Street Bump comes from its former project manager James Solomon, who was interviewed by officials from the office of the White House Chief Technology Officer.

have the effect of systematically directing city services to wealthier neighborhoods populated by smartphone owners.

To its credit, the city of Boston and the StreetBump developers figured this out before launching the app. They first deployed it to city-road inspectors, who service all parts of the city equally; the public now provides additional supporting data. It took foresight to prevent an unequal outcome, and the results were worth it. The Street Bump app has to date recorded 36,992 "bumps," helping Boston identify road castings like manholes and utility covers, not potholes, as the biggest obstacle for drivers.

More serious cases of potential discrimination occur when individuals interact with complex databases as they verify their identity. People who have multiple surnames and women who change their names when they marry typically encounter higher rates of error. This has also been true, for example, in the E-verify program, a database run jointly by the Department of Homeland Security and the Social Security Administration, which has long been a concern for civil rights advocates.

E-verify provides employers the ability to confirm the eligibility of newly hired employees to work legally in the United States. Especially given the number of queries the system processes and the volume of information it amalgamates from different sources that are themselves constantly changing, the overwhelming majority of results returned by E-verify are timely and accurate, giving employers certainty that people they hire are authorized to work in the United States. Periodic evaluations to improve the performance of E-verify have nonetheless revealed different groups receive initial verifications at different rates. A 2009 evaluation found the rate at which U.S. citizen have their authorization to work be initially erroneously unconfirmed by the system was 0.3 percent, compared to 2.1 percent for non-citizens. However, after a few days many of these workers' status was confirmed.[116]

The Department of Homeland Security and Social Security Administration have focused great attention on addressing this issue. A more recent evaluation of the program found many more people were able to verify their work status more quickly and with lower rates of error. Over five years, the rates of initial mismatch fell by 60 percent for U.S. citizens and 30 percent for non-citizens.[117] Left unresolved, technical issues like this could create higher barriers to employment or other critical needs for certain individuals and groups, making imperative the importance of accuracy, transparency, and redress in big data systems.

---

[116] Westat Corporation, *Findings of the E-Verify Program Evaluation*, December 2009, Report Submitted to Department of Homeland Security, http://www.uscis.gov/sites/default/files/USCIS/E-Verify/E-Verify/Final%20E-Verify%20Report%2012-16-09_2.pdf.

[117] Westat Corporation. *Evaluation of the Accuracy of E-Verify Findings*, July 2012, Report Submitted to Department of Homeland Security, http://www.uscis.gov/sites/default/files/USCIS/Verification/E-Verify/E-Verify_Native_Documents/Everify%20Studies/Evaluation%20of%20the%20Accuracy%20of%20EVerify%20Findings.pdf.

These two examples of inadvertent discrimination illustrate why it is important to monitor outcomes when big data technologies are applied even in instances where discriminatory intent is not present and where one might not anticipate an inequitable impact. There is, however, a whole other class that merits concern—the use of big data for deliberate discrimination.

We have taken considerable steps as a society to mandate fairness in specific domains, including employment, credit, insurance, health, housing, and education. Existing legislative and regulatory protections govern how personal data can be used in each of these contexts. Though predictive algorithms are permitted to be used in certain ways, the data that goes into them and the decisions made with their assistance are subject to some degree of transparency, correction, and means of redress. For important decisions like employment, credit, and insurance, consumers have a right to learn why a decision was made against them and what information was used to make it, and to correct the underlying information if it is in error.

These protections exist because of the United States' long history of discrimination. Since the early 20th century, banks and lenders have used location data to make assumptions about individuals. It was not until the Home Mortgage Disclosure Act was signed into law in 1975 that denying granting a person a loan on the basis of what neighborhood they live in rather than their personal capacity for credit became far less prevalent. "Redlining," in which banks quite literally drew—and in cases continue to draw—boundaries around neighborhoods where they would not loan money, existed for decades as a potent tool of discrimination against African-Americans, Latinos, Asians, and Jews.

Just as neighborhoods can serve as a proxy for racial or ethnic identity, there are new worries that big data technologies could be used to "digitally redline" unwanted groups, either as customers, employees, tenants, or recipients of credit. A significant finding of this report is that big data could enable new forms of discrimination and predatory practices.

The same algorithmic and data mining technologies that enable discrimination could also help groups enforce their rights by identifying and empirically confirming instances of discrimination and characterizing the harms they caused. Civil rights groups can use the new and powerful tools of big data in service of equal treatment for the communities they represent. Whether big data will build greater equality for all Americans or exacerbate existing inequalities depends entirely on how its technologies are applied in the years to come, what kinds of protections are present in the law, and how the law is enforced.

Big Data and Privacy

Big data technologies, together with the sensors that ride on the "Internet of Things," pierce many spaces that were previously private. Signals from home WiFi networks reveal how many people are in a room and where they are seated. Power consumption data collected from demand-response systems show when you move about your house.[118] Facial recognition technologies can identify you in pictures online and as soon as you step outside. Always-on wearable technologies with voice and video interfaces and the arrival of whole classes of networked devices will only expand information collection still further. This sea of ubiquitous sensors, each of which has legitimate uses, make the notion of limiting information collection challenging, if not impossible.

This trend toward ubiquitous collection is in part driven by the nature of technology itself.[119] Whether born analog or digital, data is being reused and combined with other data in ways never before thought possible, including for uses that go beyond the intent motivating initial collection. The potential future value of data is driving a digital land grab, shifting the priorities of organizations to collect and harness as much data as possible. Companies are now constantly looking at what kind of data they have and what data they need in order to maximize their market position. In a world where the cost of data storage has plummeted and future innovation remains unpredictable, the logic of collecting as much data as possible is strong.

Another reality of big data is that once data is collected, it can be very difficult to keep anonymous. While there are promising research efforts underway to obscure personally identifiable information within large data sets, far more advanced efforts are presently in use to re-identify seemingly "anonymous" data. Collective investment in the capability to fuse data is many times greater than investment in technologies that will enhance privacy.

Together, these trends may require us to look closely at the notice and consent framework that has been a central pillar of how privacy practices have been organized for more than four decades. In a technological context of structural over-collection, in which re-identification is becoming more powerful than de-identification, focusing on controlling the collection and retention of personal data, while important, may no longer be sufficient to protect personal privacy. In the words of the President's Council of Advisors for Science & Technology, "The notice and consent is defeated by exactly the positive benefits that big data enables: new, non-obvious, unexpectedly powerful uses of data."[120]

---

[118] Stephen Wicker and Robert Thomas, "A Privacy-Aware Architecture for Demand Response Systems," *44th Hawaii International Conference on System Sciences*, January 2011, http://ieeexplore.ieee.org/xpl/login.jsp?tp=&arnumber=5718673&url=http%3A%2F%2Fieeexplore.ieee.org%2Fxpls%2Fabs_all.jsp%3Farnumber%3D5718673; National Institute of Standards and Technology, *Guidelines for Smart Grid Cyber Security: Vol. 2, Privacy and the Smart Grid*, 2010, http://csrc.nist.gov/publications/nistir/ir7628/nistir-7628_vol2.pdf.
[119] President's Council of Advisors on Science & Technology, *Big Data and Privacy: A Technological Perspective*, The White House, May 1, 2014, whitehouse.gov/bigdata.
[120] Ibid at 36.

Federal Research in Privacy-Enhancing Technologies

The research and development of privacy enhancing technologies has been a priority for the Obama Administration. Agencies across the Networking and Information Technology Research and Development (NITRD) program collectively spend over $70 million each year on privacy research.[121] This research falls into four broad areas: support for privacy as an extension of security; research on how enterprises comply with privacy laws; privacy in health care; and basic research into technologies that enable privacy. The table below summarizes some of the research programs in progress at agencies in the NITRD. In their review of big data technologies, the President's Council of Advisors on Science & Technology endorses strengthening U.S. research in privacy-related technologies and the social science questions surrounding their use.

Research areas	Support for privacy as an extension of security	Research on how enterprises comply with privacy laws	Privacy in health care	Privacy research explorations
Agencies	Air Force Research Laboratory, Defense Advanced Research Projects Agency, National Security Agency, Intelligence Advanced Research Projects Activity, Office of Naval Research	Department of Energy, Department of Homeland Security, National Institute of Standards and Technology	Telemedicine and Advanced Technology Research Center, Office of the National Coordinator for Health Information Technology, National Institute of Health	National Science Foundation
Funding est. (total $77M/year)	$34M/year	$10M/year	$8M/year	$25M/year
Sampling of key projects	Anonymization techniques	Automated privacy compliance	Collection and use limitation	Algorithmic foundations for privacy and tools
	Confidential collaboration and communication	Location-privacy tools	Data segmentation for privacy	Economics of privacy
	Homomorphic encryption	Protection of personally identifiable information	Patient consent and privacy	Privacy as a social-psychological construct
			Patient data quality	
	Privacy preserving data aggregation	Standards for legal compliance	Preserving anonymity in health care data	Privacy policy analysis
	Traffic-secure routing	Voluntary code of conduct for smart grid		Privacy solutions for cloud computing, data integration, mining

Anticipating the Big Data Revolution's Next Chapter

For the vast majority of today's ordinary interactions between consumers and first parties, the notice and consent framework adequately safeguards privacy protections. But as the President's Council of Advisors on Science & Technology note, the trajectory of technology is shifting to far more collection, use and storage of data by entities that do

---

[121] Networking and Information Technology Research and Development, *Report on Privacy Research within NITRD,* April 2014, http://www.nitrd.gov/Pubs/Report_on_Privacy_Research_within_NITRD.pdf.

not have a direct relationship with the consumer or individual.[122] In instances where the notice and consent framework threatens to be overcome—such as the collection of ambient data by our household appliances—we may need to re-focus our attention on the context of data use, a policy shift presently being debated by privacy scholars and technologists.[123] The context of data use matters tremendously. Data that is socially beneficial in one scenario can cause significant harm in another. To borrow a term, data itself is "dual use." It can be used for good or for ill.

Putting greater emphasis on a responsible use framework has many potential advantages. It shifts the responsibility from the individual, who is not well equipped to understand or contest consent notices as they are currently structured in the marketplace, to the entities that collect, maintain, and use data. Focusing on responsible use also holds data collectors and users accountable for how they manage the data and any harms it causes, rather than narrowly defining their responsibility to whether they properly obtained consent at the time of collection.

Focusing more attention on responsible use does not mean ignoring the context of collection. Part of using data responsibly could mean respecting the circumstances of its original collection. There could, in effect, be a "no surprises" rule, as articulated in the "respect for context" principle in the Consumer Privacy Bill of Rights. Data collected in a consumer context could not suddenly be used in an employment one. Technological developments support this shift toward a focus on use. Advanced data-tagging schemes can encode details about the context of collection and uses of the data already granted by the user, so that information about permissive uses travels along with the data wherever it goes. If well developed and brought widely into use, such a data-tagging scheme would not solve all the dilemmas posed by big data, but it could help address several important challenges.

Perhaps most important of all, a shift to focus on responsible uses in the big data context allows us to put our attention more squarely on the hard questions we must reckon with: how to balance the socially beneficial uses of big data with the harms to privacy and other values that can result in a world where more data is inevitably collected about more things. Should there be an agreed-upon taxonomy that distinguishes information that you do not collect or use under any circumstances, information that you can collect or use without obtaining consent, and information that you collect and use only with consent? How should this taxonomy be different for a medical researcher trying to cure cancer and a marketer targeting ads for consumer products?

As President Obama said upon the release of the Consumer Privacy Bill of Rights, "Even though we live in a world in which we share personal information more freely than

---

[122] President's Council of Advisors on Science & Technology, *Big Data and Privacy: A Technological Perspective*, The White House, May 1, 2014, p. 20, whitehouse.gov/bigdata.
[123] Craig Mundie, "Privacy Pragmatism: Focus on Data Use, Not Data Collection," *Foreign Affairs*, March/April, 2014, http://www.foreignaffairs.com/articles/140741/craig-mundie/privacy-pragmatism.

in the past, we must reject the conclusion that privacy is an outmoded value." Privacy, the President said, "has been at the heart of our democracy from its inception, and we need it now more than ever." This is even truer in a world powered by big data.

VI. Conclusion and Recommendations

The White House review of big data and privacy, announced by President Obama on January 17, 2014, was conceived to examine the broader implications of big data technology. The President recognized the big data revolution is playing out widely across the public and private sectors and that its implications need to be considered alongside the Administration's review of signals intelligence.

The White House big data working group set out to learn, in 90 days, how big data technologies are transforming government, commerce, and society. We wanted to understand what opportunities big data affords us, and the advances it can spur. We wanted a better grasp of what kinds of technologies already existed, and what we could anticipate coming just over the horizon. The President's Council of Advisors for Science & Technology conducted a parallel report to take measure of the underlying technologies. Their findings underpin many of the technological assertions in this report.

Big data tools offer astonishing and powerful opportunities to unlock previously inaccessible insights from new and existing data sets. Big data can fuel developments and discoveries in health care and education, in agriculture and energy use, and in how businesses organize their supply chains and monitor their equipment. Big data holds the potential to streamline the provision of public services, increase the efficient use of taxpayer dollars at every level of government, and substantially strengthen national security. The promise of big data requires government data be viewed as a national resource and be responsibly made available to those who can derive social value from it. It also presents the opportunity to shape the next generation of computational tools and technologies that will in turn drive further innovation.

Big data also introduces many quandaries. By their very nature, many of the sensor technologies deployed on our phones and in our homes, offices, and on lampposts and rooftops across our cities are collecting more and more information. Continuing advances in analytics provide incentives to collect as much data as possible not only for today's uses but also for potential later uses. Technologically speaking, this is driving data collection to become functionally ubiquitous and permanent, allowing the digital traces we leave behind to be collected, analyzed, and assembled to reveal a surprising number of things about ourselves and our lives. These developments challenge longstanding notions of privacy and raise questions about the "notice and consent" framework, by which a user gives initial permission for their data to be collected. But these trends need not prevent creating ways for people to participate in the treatment and management of their information.

An important finding of this review is that while big data can be used for great social good, it can also be used in ways that perpetrate social harms or render outcomes that have inequitable impacts, even when discrimination is not intended. Small biases have the potential to become cumulative, affecting a wide range of outcomes for certain disadvantaged groups. Society must take steps to guard against these potential harms by ensuring power is appropriately balanced between individuals and institutions, whether between citizen and government, consumer and firm, or employee and business.

The big data revolution is in its earliest stages. We will be grappling for many years to understand the full sweep of its technologies; the ways it will empower health, education, and the economy; and, crucially, what its implications are for core American values, including privacy, fairness, non-discrimination, and self-determination.

Even at this early juncture, the authors of this report believe important conclusions are already emerging about big data that can inform how the Administration moves forward in a number of areas. In particular, there are five areas that will each bring the American people into the national conversation about how to maximize benefits and minimize harms in a big data world:

1. **Preserving Privacy Values:** Maintaining our privacy values by protecting personal information in the marketplace, both in the United States and through interoperable global privacy frameworks;

2. **Educating Robustly and Responsibly:** Recognizing schools—particularly K-12—as an important sphere for using big data to enhance learning opportunities, while protecting personal data usage and building digital literacy and skills;

3. **Big Data and Discrimination:** Preventing new modes of discrimination that some uses of big data may enable;

4. **Law Enforcement and Security:** Ensuring big data's responsible use in law enforcement, public safety, and national security; and

5. **Data as a Public Resource:** Harnessing data as a public resource, using it to improve the delivery of public services, and investing in research and technology that will further power the big data revolution.

Policy Recommendations:

This review also identifies six discrete policy recommendations that deserve prompt Administration attention and policy development. These are:

- **Advance the Consumer Privacy Bill of Rights.** The Department of Commerce should take appropriate consultative steps to seek stakeholder and public comment on big data developments and how they impact the Consumer Privacy Bill of Rights and then devise draft legislative text for consideration by stakeholders and submission by the President to Congress.

- **Pass National Data Breach Legislation.** Congress should pass legislation that provides for a single national data breach standard along the lines of the Administration's May 2011 Cybersecurity legislative proposal.

- **Extend Privacy Protections to non-U.S. Persons.** The Office of Management and Budget should work with departments and agencies to apply the Privacy Act of 1974 to non-U.S. persons where practicable, or to establish alternative privacy policies that apply appropriate and meaningful protections to personal information regardless of a person's nationality.

- **Ensure Data Collected on Students in School is Used for Educational Purposes.** The federal government must ensure that privacy regulations protect students against having their data being shared or used inappropriately, especially when the data is gathered in an educational context.

- **Expand Technical Expertise to Stop Discrimination.** The federal government's lead civil rights and consumer protection agencies should expand their technical expertise to be able to identify practices and outcomes facilitated by big data analytics that have a discriminatory impact on protected classes, and develop a plan for investigating and resolving violations of law.

- **Amend the Electronic Communications Privacy Act.** Congress should amend ECPA to ensure the standard of protection for online, digital content is consistent with that afforded in the physical world—including by removing archaic distinctions between email left unread or over a certain age.

1. Preserving Privacy Values

Big data technologies are driving enormous innovation while raising novel privacy implications that extend far beyond the present focus on online advertising. These implications make urgent a broader national examination of the future of privacy protections, including the Administration's Consumer Privacy Bill of Rights, released in 2012. It will be especially important to re-examine the traditional notice and consent framework that focuses on obtaining user permission prior to collecting data. While notice and consent remains fundamental in many contexts, it is now necessary to examine whether a greater focus on how data is used and reused would be a more productive basis for managing privacy rights in a big data environment. It may be that creating mechanisms for individuals to participate in the use and distribution of his or her information after it is collected is actually a better and more empowering way to allow people to access the benefits that derive from their information. Privacy protections must also evolve in a way that accommodates the social good that can come of big data use.

Advance the Consumer Privacy Bill of Rights

As President Obama made clear in February 2012, the Consumer Privacy Bill of Rights and the associated Blueprint for Consumer Privacy represent "a dynamic model of how to offer strong privacy protection and enable ongoing innovation in new information technologies." The Consumer Privacy Bill of Rights is based on the Fair Information Practice Principles. Some privacy experts believe nuanced articulations of these principles are flexible enough to address and support new and emerging uses of data, including big data. Others, especially technologists, are less sure, as it is undeniable that big data challenges several of the key assumptions that underpin current privacy frameworks, especially around collection and use. These big data developments warrant consideration in the context of how to viably ensure privacy protection and what practical limits exist to the practice of notice and consent.

> **RECOMMENDATION:** *The Department of Commerce should promptly seek public comment on how the Consumer Privacy Bill of Rights could support the innovations of big data while at the same time responding to its risks, and how a responsible use framework, as articulated in Chapter 5, could be embraced within the framework established by the Consumer Privacy Bill of Rights. Following the comment process, the Department of Commerce should work on draft legislative text for consideration by stakeholders and for submission by the President to Congress.*

Pass national data breach legislation to benefit consumers and businesses

As organizations store more information about individuals, Americans have a right to know if that information has been stolen or otherwise improperly exposed. A patchwork of 47 state laws currently governs when and how the loss of personally identifiable information must be reported.

> RECOMMENDATION: *Congress should pass legislation that provides for a single national data breach standard along the lines of the Administration's May 2011 Cybersecurity legislative proposal. Such legislation should impose reasonable time periods for notification, minimize interference with law enforcement investigations, and potentially prioritize notification about large, damaging incidents over less significant incidents.*

The data services industry—colloquially known as "data brokers"—should bring greater transparency to the sector

Consumers deserve more transparency about how their data is shared beyond the entities with which they do business directly, including "third-party" data collectors. This means ensuring that consumers are meaningfully aware of the spectrum of information collection and reuse as the number of firms that are involved in mediating their consumer experience or collecting information from them multiplies. The data services industry should follow the lead of the online advertising and credit industries and build a common website or online portal that lists companies, describes their data practices, and provides methods for consumers to better control how their information is collected and used or to opt-out of certain marketing uses.

Even as we focus more on data use, consumers still have a valid interest in "Do Not Track" tools that help them control when and how their data is collected.

Strengthening these tools is especially important because there is now a growing array of technologies available for recording individual actions, behavior, and location data across a range of services and devices. Public surveys indicate a clear and overwhelming demand for these tools, and the government and private sector must continue working to evolve privacy-enhancing technologies in step with improved consumer services.

The government should lead a consultative process to assess how the Health Insurance Portability and Accountability Act and other relevant federal laws and regulations can best accommodate the advances in medical science and cost reduction in health care delivery enabled by big data

Breakthroughs in predicting, detecting, and treating disease deserve the utmost public policy attention, but are unlikely to realize their full potential without substantial improvements in the medical data privacy regime that enables researchers to combine and analyze various kinds of lifestyle and health information. Any proposed reform must also consider bringing under regulatory and legal protection the vast quantities of personal health information circulated by organizations that are not covered entities governed by the Health Insurance Portability and Accountability Act.

The United States should lead international conversations on big data that reaffirms the Administration's commitment to interoperable global privacy frameworks

The benefits of big data depend on the global free flow of information. The United States should engage international partners in a dialogue on the benefits and challenges of big data as they impact the legal frameworks and traditions of different nations.

Specifically, the Department of State and the Department of Commerce should actively engage with bilateral and intergovernmental partners, including the European Union, Asia Pacific Economic Cooperation (APEC), and Organization for Economic Cooperation and Development, and with other stakeholders, to take stock of how existing and proposed policy frameworks address big data.

The Administration should also work to strengthen the U.S.-European Union Safe Harbor Framework, encourage more countries and companies to join the APEC Cross Border Privacy Rules system, and promote collaboration on data flows between the United States, Europe and Asia through efforts to align Europe's system of Binding Corporate Rules and the APEC CBPR system.

Privacy is a worldwide value that the United States respects and which should be reflected in how it handles data regarding all persons

For this reason the United States should extend privacy protections to non-U.S. persons.

RECOMMENDATION: *The Office of Management and Budget should work with departments and agencies to apply the Privacy Act of 1974 to non-U.S. persons where practicable, or to establish alternative privacy policies that apply appropriate and meaningful protections to personal information regardless of a person's nationality.*

2. Responsible Educational Innovation in the Digital Age

Big data offers significant opportunities to improve learning experiences for children and young adults. Big data intersects with education in two important ways. As students begin to share information with educational institutions, they expect that they are doing so in order to develop knowledge and skills, not to have their data used to build extensive profiles about their strengths and weaknesses that could be used to their disadvantage in later years. Educational institutions are also in a unique position to help prepare children, adolescents, and adults to grapple with the world of big data.

Ensure data protection while promoting innovation in learning

Substantial breakthroughs stand to be made using big data to improve education as personalized learning on network-enabled devices becomes more common. Over the next five years, under the President's ConnectED initiative, American classrooms will receive a dramatic influx of technology—with substantial potential to enhance teaching and learning, particularly for disadvantaged communities. Internet-based education tools and software enable rapid iteration and innovation in educational technologies and businesses. These technologies are already being deployed with strong privacy and safety protections for students, inside and outside of the classroom. The Family Educational Rights and Privacy Act and Children's Online Privacy Protection Act provide a federal regulatory framework to protect the privacy of students—but FERPA was written before the Internet, and COPPA was written before smartphones, tablets, apps, the cloud, and big data. Students and their families need robust protection against current and emerging harms, but they also deserve access to the learning advancements enabled by technology that promise to empower all students to reach their full potential.

> RECOMMENDATION: *The federal government should ensure that data collected in schools is used for educational purposes and continue to support investment and innovation that raises the level of performance across our schools. To promote this innovation, it should explore how to modernize the privacy regulatory framework under the Family Educational Rights and Privacy Act and Children's Online Privacy Protection Act and Children's Online Privacy Protection Act to ensure two complementary goals: 1) protecting students against their data being shared or used inappropriately, especially when that data is gathered in an educational context, and 2) ensuring that innovation in educational technology, including new approaches and business models, have ample opportunity to flourish.*

Recognize digital literacy as an important 21st century skill.

In order to ensure students, citizens, and consumers of all ages have the ability to adequately protect themselves from data use and abuse, it is important that they develop fluency in understanding the ways in which data can be collected and shared, how algorithms are employed and for what purposes, and what tools and techniques they can use to protect themselves. Although such skills will never replace regulatory protections, increased digital literacy will better prepare individuals to live in a world saturated by data. Digital literacy—understanding how personal data is collected, shared, and used—should be recognized as an essential skill in K-12 education and be integrated into the standard curriculum.

3. Big Data and Discrimination

The technologies of automated decision-making are opaque and largely inaccessible to the average person. Yet they are assuming increasing importance and being used in contexts related to individuals' access to health, education, employment, credit, and goods and services. This combination of circumstances and technology raises difficult questions about how to ensure that discriminatory effects resulting from automated decision processes, whether intended or not, can be detected, measured, and redressed. We must begin a national conversation on big data, discrimination, and civil liberties.

The federal government must pay attention to the potential for big data technologies to facilitate discrimination inconsistent with the country's laws and values

> **RECOMMENDATION:** *The federal government's lead civil rights and consumer protection agencies, including the Department of Justice, the Federal Trade Commission, the Consumer Financial Protection Bureau, and the Equal Employment Opportunity Commission, should expand their technical expertise to be able to identify practices and outcomes facilitated by big data analytics that have a discriminatory impact on protected classes, and develop a plan for investigating and resolving violations of law in such cases. In assessing the potential concerns to address, the agencies may consider the classes of data, contexts of collection, and segments of the population that warrant particular attention, including for example genomic information or information about people with disabilities.*

Consumers have a legitimate expectation of knowing whether the prices they are offered for goods and services are systematically different than the prices offered to others

It is implausible for consumers to be presented with the full parameters of the data and algorithms shaping their online and offline experience. Nonetheless, some transparency is appropriate when a consumer's experience is being altered based on their personal information, particularly in situations where companies offer differential pricing to consumers in situations where they would not expect it—such as when comparing airline ticket prices on a web-based search engine or visiting the online storefront of a major retailer. The President's Council of Economic Advisers should assess the evolving practices of differential pricing both online and offline, assess the implications for efficient operations of markets, and consider whether new practices are needed to ensure fairness for the consumer.

Data analytics can be used to shore up civil liberties

The same big data technologies that enable discrimination can also help groups enforce their rights. Applying correlative and data mining capabilities can identify and empirically confirm instances of discrimination and characterize the harms they caused. The federal government's civil rights offices, together with the civil rights community, should employ the new and powerful tools of big data to ensure that our most vulnerable communities are treated fairly.

To build public awareness, the federal government's consumer protection and technology agencies should convene public workshops and issue reports over the next year on the potential for discriminatory practices in light of these new technologies; differential pricing practices; and the use of proxy scoring to replicate regulated scoring practices in credit, employment, education, housing, and health care.

4. Law Enforcement and Security

Big data, lawfully applied, can make our communities safer, make our nation's infrastructure more resilient, and strengthen our national security. It is crucial that the national security, homeland security, law enforcement, and intelligence communities continue to vigorously experiment with and apply lawful big data technology while adhering to full accountability, oversight, and relevant privacy requirements.

The Electronic Communications Privacy Act should be reformed

RECOMMENDATION: *Congress should amend ECPA to ensure the standard of protection for online, digital content is consistent with that afforded in the physical world—including by removing archaic distinctions between email left unread or over a certain age.*

The use of predictive analytics by law enforcement should continue to be subjected to careful policy review

It is essential that big data analysis conducted by law enforcement outside the context of predicated criminal investigations be deployed with appropriate protections for individual privacy and civil liberties. The presumption of innocence is the bedrock of the American criminal justice system. To prevent chilling effects to Constitutional rights of free speech and association, the public must be aware of the existence, operation, and efficacy of such programs.

Federal agencies with expertise in privacy and data practices should provide technical assistance to state, local, and other federal law enforcement agencies seeking to deploy big data techniques

Law enforcement agencies should continue to examine how federal grants involving big data surveillance technologies can foster their responsible use, as well as the potential utility of establishing a national registry of big data pilots in state and local law enforcement in order to track, identify, and promote best practices. Federal government agencies with technology leaders and experts should also report progress in developing privacy-protective technologies over the next year to help advance the development of technical skills for the advancement of the federal privacy community.

Government use of lawfully-acquired commercial data should be evaluated to ensure consistency with our values

Recognizing the longstanding practice of basic commercial records searches against criminal suspects, the federal government should undertake a review of uses of commercially available data on U.S. citizens, focusing on the use of services that employ big data techniques and ensuring that they incorporate appropriate oversight and protections for privacy and civil liberties.

Federal agencies should implement best practices for institutional protocols and mechanisms that can help ensure the controlled use and secure storage of data

The Department of Homeland Security, the intelligence community, and the Department of Defense are among the leaders in developing privacy-protective technologies and policies for handling personal data. Other public sector agencies should evaluate whether any of these practices—particularly data tagging to enforce usage limitations, controlled access policies, and immutable auditing—could be integrated into their databases and data practices to provide built-in protections for privacy, civil rights, and civil liberties.

Use big data analysis and information sharing to strengthen cybersecurity

Protecting the networks that drive our economy, sustain public safety, and protect our national security has become a critical homeland security mission. The federal government's collaboration with private sector partners to use big data in programs, pilots, and research for both cybersecurity and protecting critical infrastructure can help strengthen our resilience and cyber defenses, especially as more cyber threat data is shared. The Administration continues to support legislation that protects privacy while providing targeted liability protection for companies sharing certain threat information and appropriately defending their networks on that basis. At the same time, the Administration will continue to use executive action to increase incentives for and reduce barriers to the kind of information sharing and analytics that will help the public and private sector prevent and respond to cyber threats.

5. Data as a Public Resource

Government data is a national resource, and should be made broadly available to the public wherever possible, to advance government efficiency, ensure government accountability, and generate economic prosperity and social good—while continuing to protect personal privacy, business confidentiality, and national security. This means finding new opportunities for the government to release large data sets and ensuring all agencies make maximum use of Data.gov, a repository of federal data tools and resources. Big data can help improve the provision of public services, provide new insights to inform policymaking, and increase the efficient use of taxpayer dollars at every level of government.

Government data should be accurate and securely stored, and to the maximum extent possible, open and accessible

Government data—particularly statistical and census data—distinguishes itself by providing a high level of accuracy, reliability, and confidentiality. Similarly, the "My Data" initiatives that currently allow Americans easy, secure access to their own digital data in useful formats constitutes a model for personal data accessibility that should be replicated as widely as possible across the government.

All departments and agencies should, in close coordination with their senior privacy and civil liberties officials, examine how they might best harness big data to help carry out their missions

Departments and agencies that have not historically made wide use of advanced data analytics should make the most out of what the big data revolution means for them and the citizens they serve. They should experiment with pilot projects, develop in-house talent, and potentially expand research and development. From the earliest stages, agencies should build these projects in consultation with their privacy and civil liberties officers.

In particular, big data analytics present an important opportunity to increase value and performance for the American people in the delivery of government services. Big data also holds enormous power to detect and address waste, fraud and abuse, thereby saving taxpayer money and improving public trust. Big data can further help identify high performers across government whose practices can be replicated by similar agencies and programs and may deliver new insights into effective public-sector management.

We should dramatically increase investment for research and development in privacy-enhancing technologies, encouraging cross-cutting research that involves not only computer science and mathematics, but also social science, communications and legal disciplines

The Administration should lead an effort to identify areas where big data analytics can provide the greatest impact for improving the lives of Americans and encourage data scientists to develop social, ethical, and policy knowledge. To this end, the Office of Science and Technology Policy, in partnership with experts across the agencies, should work to define areas that promise significant public gains—for example, in urban informatics—and assess how to provide appropriate attention and resources.

Promising areas for basic research include data provenance, de-identification and encryption, but we also encourage focusing on lab-to-market tools that can be rapidly deployed to consumers. Because we will need a growing cadre of data and social scientists who are able to encode critical policy values into technical infrastructure, we support investment in fields such as Science and Technology Studies which emphasize teaching scientific knowledge and technology in its social and ethical context, and the teaching of module courses to data scientists and engineers to familiarize them with the broader societal implications of their work.

Appendix

Index

A. Methodology

This 90-day study was announced by President Obama in his January 17, 2014 remarks on the review of signals intelligence. He charged his Counselor John Podesta to "look how the challenges inherent in big data are being confronted by both the public and private sectors; whether we can forge international norms on how to manage this data; and how we can continue to promote the free flow of information in ways that are consistent with both privacy and security." Podesta led a working group of senior Administration officials including Secretary of Commerce Penny Pritzker, Secretary of Energy Ernie Moniz, Director of the Office of Science and Technology Policy John Holdren, and Director of the National Economic Council Jeffrey Zients. Nicole Wong, R. David Edelman, Christopher Kirchhoff, and Kristina Costa were the principal staff authors supporting this report. To inform its deliberations, the working group initiated a broad public dialogue on the implications of technological advancements in big data.

During the course of this study, the working group met with hundreds of stakeholders from industry, academia, civil society, and the federal government through briefings at the White House. These briefings provided a chance for dialogue with key stakeholders, including privacy and civil liberties advocates; scientific and statistical agencies; international data protection authorities; the intelligence community; law enforcement officials; leading academics who study social and technical aspects of privacy and the Internet; and practitioners and executives from the health care, financial, and information services industries. A full list of briefings and participants is included in Section B of the appendix.

To further engage the public, the White House Office of Science and Technology Policy sponsored conferences at the Massachusetts Institute of Technology, New York University, and the University of California, Berkeley. Senior Administration officials, including Counselor Podesta and Secretary Pritzker, participated in these conferences, along with policy experts, academics, and representatives from business and the nonprofit community. Details of these conferences and a list of presentations is included in Section C of the appendix.

The working group also published a Federal Register notice to gather written input, and used the whitehouse.gov platform to solicit comments from the general public online. Details of these efforts are included in Sections E and F of the appendix.

B. Stakeholder Meetings

Acxiom
Adobe
Allstate
Ally Financial
Amazon
American Association of Advertising Agencies
American Association of Universities
American Civil Liberties Union
Apple
AppNexus
Archimedes Incorporated
Asian Americans Advancing Justice
Association of National Advertisers
athenahealth
Bank of America
BlueKai
Bureau of Consumer Protection
Canadian Interim Privacy Commissioner
Capital One
Carnegie Mellon University
Cato Institute
Census Bureau
Center for Democracy & Technology
Center for Digital Democracy
Center for National Security Studies
Central Intelligence Agency
ColorOfChange
Computer Science and Artificial Intelligence Laboratory, MIT
comScore
Corelogic
Cornell University
Council of Better Business Bureaus
Datalogix
Department of Commerce, General Counsel
Department of Homeland Security
Digital Advertising Alliance
Direct Marketing Association

Discover
Drug Enforcement Administration
Duke University School of Law
Dutch Data Protection Authority
Economics and Statistics Administration
Electronic Frontier Foundation
Electronic Privacy Information Center
Epsilon
European Union Data Protection Supervisor
European Commission: Directorate-General for Justice (Data Protection Division)
Evidera
Experian
Explorys
Facebook
Federal Bureau of Investigation
Federal Telecommunications Commission, Bureau of Consumer Protection
Financial Services Roundtable
Free Press
French National Commission on Informatics and Liberty
Future of Privacy
George Washington University
Georgetown University Law Center
GNS Health care
Google
GroupM
Harvard University
Humedica
IBM Health care
IMS Health
Infogroup
Interactive Advertising Bureau
International Association of Privacy Professionals
Jenner & Block LLP
Lawrence Berkeley National Laboratory
Lawrence Livermore National Laboratory
LexisNexis
LinkedIn
Massachusetts Institute of Technology
Massachusetts Institute of Technology Media Lab
MasterCard
Mexican Data Privacy Commissioner
Microsoft
National Association for the Advancement of Colored People
National Economic Council
National Hispanic Media Coalition
National Oceanic and Atmospheric Administration
National Organization for Women
National Security Agency
National Telecommunications and Information Administration
National Urban League Policy Institute

NaviMed Capital
Network Advertising Initiative
Neustar
Office of Chairwoman Edith Ramirez
Office of Science and Technology Policy
Office of the Director of National Intelligence
Office of the National Coordinator for Health Information Technology
Ogilvy
Open Society Foundations
Open Technology Institute
Optum Labs
PatientsLikeMe
Princeton University
Privacy Analytics
Public Knowledge
Quantcast
Robinson & Yu LLC
SalesForce
The Brookings Institution
The Constitution Project
The Leadership Conference on Civil and Human Rights
UK Information Commissioner
University of Maryland
University of Virginia
Visa
Yahoo!
Zillow

C. Academic Symposia

Big Data and Privacy Workshop: Advancing the State of the Art in Technology and Practice
Massachusetts Institute of Technology (MIT)
Cambridge, Massachusetts
March 3, 2014

Welcome: L. Rafael Reif, President of MIT

Keynote: John Podesta, Counselor to the President

Keynote: Penny Pritzker, Secretary of Commerce

State of the Art of Privacy Protection: Cynthia Dwork, Microsoft

Panel Session 1: Big Data Opportunities and Challenges
     Panel Chair: Daniela Rus, MIT
     Mike Stonebraker, MIT
     John Guttag, MIT
     Manolis Kellis, MIT
     Sam Madden, MIT
     Anant Agarwal, edX

Panel Session 2: Privacy Enhancing Technologies
     Panel Chair: Shafi Goldwasser
     Nickolai Zeldovich, MIT
     Vinod Vaikuntanathan, Assistant Professor, MIT
     Salil Vadhan, Harvard University
     Daniel Weitzner, MIT

Panel Session 3: Roundtable Discussion of Large-Scale Analytics Case Study
     Panel Moderator: Daniel Weitzner
     Chris Calabrese, American Civil Liberties Union
     John DeLong, National Security Agency
     Mark Gorenberg, Zetta Venture Partners
     David Hoffman, Intel
     Karen Kornbluh, Nielsen
     Andy Palmer, KOA Lab
     James Powell, Thomson Reuters
     Latanya Sweeney, Harvard University
     Vinod Vaikuntanathan, MIT

Concluding Statements: Maria Zuber, MIT

The Social, Cultural, & Ethical Dimensions of 'Big Data'
The Data & Society Research Institute & New York University (NYU)
New York, New York
March 17, 2014

Introduction: danah boyd, Data & Society

Fireside Chat: John Podesta, Counselor to the President

Keynote: Penny Pritzker, Secretary of Commerce

State of the Art of Privacy Protection: Cynthia Dwork, Microsoft

Discussion Breakouts
     Tim Hwang: On Cognitive Security
     Nick Grossman: Regulation 2.0
     Nuala O'Connor: The Digital Self & Technology in Daily Life
     Alex Howard: Data Journalism in the Second Machine Age
     Mark Latonero: Big Data and Human Trafficking
     Corrine Yu: Civil Rights Principles for the Era of Big Data
     Natasha Schüll: Tracking for Profit; Tracking for Protection
     Kevin Bankston: The Biggest Data of All
     Alessandro Acquisti: The Economics of Privacy (and Big Data)
     Latanya Sweeney: Transparency Builds Trust
     Deborah Estrin: You + Your Data
     Clay Shirky: Analog Thumbs on Digital Scales Open Discussion
     Moderators: danah boyd and Nicole Wong

Workshops
     Data Supply Chains
     Inferences and Connections
     Predicting Human Behavior
     Algorithmic Accountability
     Interpretation Gone Wrong
     Inequalities and Asymmetries

Public Plenary
     Welcome: danah boyd, Data & Society
     Video Address: John Podesta, Counselor to the President
     Keynote: Nicole Wong, Deputy Chief Technology Officer of the US
     Plenary Panel Statements
          Kate Crawford, Microsoft Research and MIT
          Anil Dash, Think Up and Activate (moderator)
          Steven Hodas, NYC Department of Education
          Alondra Nelson, Columbia University
          Shamina Singh, MasterCard Center for Inclusive Growth

Big Data: Values and Governance
University of California, Berkeley (UC Berkeley)
Berkeley, California
April 1, 2014

Welcome: Dean AnnaLee Saxenian, UC Berkeley School of Information

Welcome: Nicole Wong, Deputy Chief Technology Officer, OSTP

Panel Session 1: Values at stake, Values in tension: Privacy and Beyond
    Moderator: Deirdre Mulligan, UC Berkeley School of Information
    Amalia Deloney, Center for Media Justice
    Nicole Ozer, Northern California ACLU
    Fred Cate, University of Indiana
    Kenneth A. Bamberger, UC Berkeley School of Law

Panel Session 2: New Opportunities and Challenges in Health and Education
    Moderator: Paul Ohm, University of Colorado Law School
    Barbara Koenig, University of California, San Francisco
    Deven McGraw, Center for Democracy & Technology
    Scott Young, Kaiser Permanente
    Zachary Pardos, UC Berkeley School of Information

Panel Session 3: Algorithms: Transparency, Accountability, Values and Discretion
    Moderator: Omer Tene, International Association of Privacy Professionals
    Ari Gesher, Palantir
    Lee Tien, Electronic Frontier Foundation
    Seeta Gangadharan, New America Foundation
    Thejo Kote, Automatic
    James Rule, UC Berkeley

Governance Roundtable
    Moderator: David Vladeck, Georgetown University Law School
    Julie Brill, Federal Trade Commission
    Erika Rottenberg, LinkedIn
    Cameron Kerry, MIT Media Lab
    Cynthia Dwork, Microsoft Research
    Mitchell Stevens, Stanford University
    Rainer Stentzel, German Federal Ministry of the Interior

Concluding Keynote: John Podesta, Counselor to the President

D. PCAST Report

To take measure of the shifting technological landscape, the President charged his Council of Advisors on Science & Technology (PCAST) to conduct a parallel study to assess the technological dimensions of the intersection of big data and privacy. PCAST's statement of work reads, in part:

> "PCAST will study the technological aspects of the intersection of big data with individual privacy, in relation to both the current state and possible future states of the relevant technological capabilities and associated privacy concerns.

> Relevant big data include data and metadata collected, or potentially collectable, from or about individuals by entities that include the government, the private sector, and other individuals. It includes both proprietary and open data, and also data about individuals collected incidentally or accidentally in the course of other activities (e.g., environmental monitoring or the "Internet of things").

The PCAST assessment was conducted simultaneously with the 90-study on big data. PCAST shared their preliminary conclusions with the working group in order to inform its deliberations. The final PCAST report can be found at whitehouse.gov/bigdata and at PCAST's own website, whitehouse.gov/administration/eop/ostp/pcast.

E. Public Request for Information

As part of the effort to make this review as inclusive as possible, the White House Office of Science and Technology Policy (OSTP) released a Request for Information (RFI) seeking public comment on the ways in which big data may impact privacy, the economy, and public policy. The RFI was published on March 4, 2014, and 76 comments were submitted through April 4, 2014. The comments came from nonprofits, corporations, universities, and individual citizens. The full list of respondents is included below, and the full text of all responses is publicly available at whitehouse.gov/bigdata.

The RFI posed five questions to respondents:

> (1) What are the public policy implications of the collection, storage, analysis, and use of big data? For example, do the current U.S. policy framework and privacy proposals for protecting consumer privacy and government use of data adequately address issues raised by big data analytics?

> (2) What types of uses of big data could measurably improve outcomes or productivity with further government action, funding, or research? What types of uses of big data raise the most public policy concerns? Are there specific sectors or types of uses that should receive more government and/or public attention?

> (3) What technological trends or key technologies will affect the collection, storage, analysis and use of big data? Are there particularly promising technologies or new practices for safeguarding privacy while enabling effective uses of big data?

> (4) How should the policy frameworks or regulations for handling big data differ between the government and the private sector? Please be specific as to the type of entity and type of use (e.g., law enforcement, government services, commercial, academic research, etc.).

(5) What issues are raised by the use of big data across jurisdictions, such as the adequacy of current international laws, regulations, or norms?

The RFI can be found at:
http://www.gpo.gov/fdsys/pkg/FR-2014-03-04/pdf/2014-04660.pdf.

Respondents:

Access
American Civil Liberties Union
Ad Self-Regulatory Council, Council of Better Business Bureaus
Annie Shebanow
The Architecture for a Digital World and Advanced Micro Devices
Association for Computing Machinery
Association of National Advertisers
Brennan Center for Justice
BSA | The Software Alliance
Center for Democracy and Technology
Center for Data Innovation
Center for Digital Democracy
Center for National Security Studies
Cloud Security Alliance
Coalition for Privacy and Free Trade
Common Sense Media
Computer and Communications Industry Association
Computing Community Consortium
Constellation Research
Consumer Action
Consumer Federation of America
Consumer Watchdog
Dell
Direct Marketing Association
Dr. Tyrone W A Grandison
Dr. A. R. Wagner
Durrell Kapan
Electronic Frontier Foundation
Electronic Transactions Association
Entity
Federation of American Societies for Experimental Biology
Financial Services Roundtable
Food Marketing Groups
Frank Pasquale, UMD Law
Fred Cate, Microsoft, Oxford Internet Institute
Future of Privacy Forum
Georgetown University
Health care Leadership Council
IMS Health
Information Technology Industry Council
Interactive Advertising Bureau
Intrical

IT Law Group
Jackamo
James Cooper, George Mason Law
Jason Kint
Jonathan Sander, STEALTHbits
Kaliya Identity Woman
Leadership Conferences on Civil and Human Rights & Education
Making Change at Walmart
Marketing Research Association
Mary Culnan, Bentley University & Future of Privacy Forum
McKenna Long & Aldridge LLP
mediajustice.org
Microsoft
Massachusetts Institute of Technology
MITRE Corporation
Mozilla
New York University Center for Urban Science & Progress
Online Trust Alliance
Pacific Northwest National Laboratory
Peter Muhlberger
Privacy Coalition
Reed Elsevier
Sidley Austin LLP
Software & Information Industry Association
TechAmerica
TechFreedom
Technology Policy Institute
The Internet Association
U.S. Chamber of Commerce
U.S. Leadership for the Revision of the 1967 Space Treaty
U.S. PIRG
VIPR Systems
World Privacy Forum

F. White House Big Data Survey

Additional public input about big data and privacy issues was solicited via a short web form posted on WhiteHouse.gov and promoted via email and social media. During the four weeks the survey was open for public input, 24,092 people submitted responses. It is important to note, however, that this process was a means of gathering public input and should not be considered a statistically representative survey of attitudes about data privacy. The White House did not include submission fields for name or contact information on the survey form.

Respondents expressed a great deal of concern about big data practices. They communicated particularly strong feelings around ensuring that data practices have proper transparency and oversight—more than 80 percent of respondents were very concerned with each of these areas—but even in the area of least concern (collection of location data), 61 percent indicated that they were "very much concerned" about this practice. By contrast, considerably more nuance was evident in respondents' views towards particular entities. Although majorities claimed to trust Intelligence and Law Enforcement Agencies "not at all," their views towards other government agencies at both federal and local levels were far less negative. Furthermore, majorities were generally trusting of how professional practices, like law and medical offices, and academia use and handle big data.

Concern with data practices

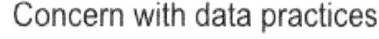

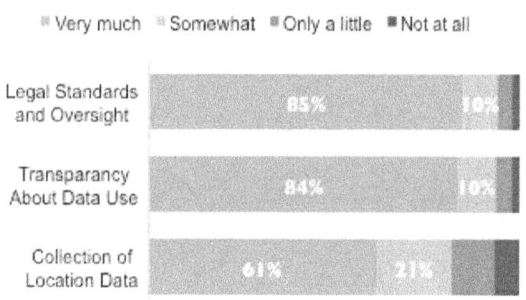

Percent who do not trust each entity at all

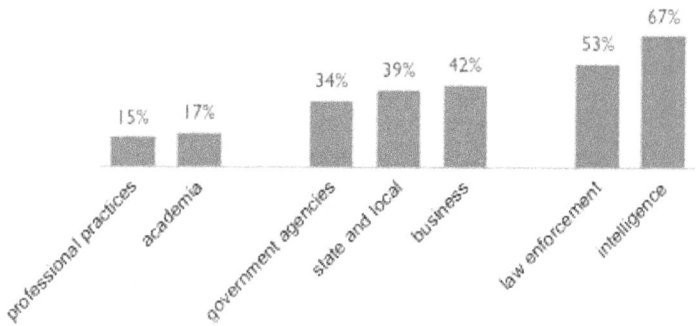

Taken together, the findings from this survey indicate that respondents were most wary of how intelligence and law enforcement agencies are collecting and using data about them, particularly when they have little insight into these practices. This suggests that the Administration should work to increase the transparency about intelligence practices where possible, reassure the public that collected data is stored as securely as possible, and strengthen applicable legal structures and oversight.

For more information about the survey, visit: WhiteHouse.gov/BigData.